The Journalist's Handbook

TONBRIDGE SCHOOL
ENGLISH DEPARTMENT

The
Journalist's
Handbook

Christopher Browne

A&C Black · London

First published in 1999
by A & C Black (Publishers) Limited
35 Bedford Row, London WC1R 4JH

ISBN 0-7136-4949-6

A CIP catalogue record for this book is available from the British Library.

Cover photograph: PA News

Typeset in New Century Schoolbook
Designed and produced by Sandie Boccacci
Printed and bound in Great Britain by
Creative Print and Design (Wales), Ebbw Vale

Contents

Acknowledgements

The publishers wish to acknowledge the following for permission to use extracts/pictures:

The Daily Mail (p. 133)
The Evening Standard (p. 99)
Express Newspapers (p. 66)
Stuart Hiern-Cooke (p. 113)
The Independent, Andrew Verity and Paul Waugh (p. 127)
The Sun (p. 117, p. 133)
Times Newspapers Ltd (p. 117, p. 133)

The Publisher has made every effort to contact the copyright holders of the text extracts used in this book. In some cases this has not proved possible and the Publisher apologises to any copyright holder whose work has been used without specific permission.

About the author

Christopher Browne is a national newspaper journalist, who has worked on *The Times*, *Sunday Times* and *Daily Telegraph*. He also broadcasts regularly on such key media issues as intrusion, privacy, human rights and the freedom of the press.

By the same author
Getting The Message: the story of the Post Office
The Prying Game: the power of the media

Preface

Journalists are the hardest-working lazy people in the world; this was the view of the writer G.K. Chesterton. He was probably right. Most journalists have an idle streak piercing their scaly veneers.

Lord Northcliffe, founder of *The Mirror*, carried the idea further. Shortly before he went mad and died, he said journalism was a 'profession whose business it is to explain to others what it personally does not understand'.

Feckless and lazy they may be. But journalists are also doers and the way to get on in the media is to practise it, to interview people, to visit and write about events, to conjure up ideas and to write articles for any publication you come across from college newsletter to local magazine.

The way *not* to get on is to bamboozle yourself into thinking that reading reams of knowledge and theory, or boasting that you want to be a journalist to your friends, will turn you into a super-sleuth.

This book is not a dry polemic but aims to help create the embryo of the journalist and guide his/her first halting steps into the mediascape.

If a student asks me how to make it, I say quite simply: 'Put yourself about, offer to do work experience wherever you can, choose the niche you want to specialise in, and build up a network of contacts.' That way you will quickly become the master of your own destiny.

At the deciding stage, talk to as many people as you can in your chosen field of print, broadcasting or PR. Ask them how they got there, what tips they can pass on and whether they know of any useful sources for jobs or training.

Talk to potential employers. If necessary, go and see them and present them with a neat pile of cuttings of work from school, college or university. Most of all, be enthusiastic and determined.

It is up to you to prove Chesterton's theory of hard-working idleness correct!

CHRISTOPHER BROWNE
Twickenham,
July 1999

I would like to thank the students on my journalism training courses who taught me everything I know.

Introduction

I WANT TO BE A JOURNALIST

If you go to a party and say you're a journalist, a group of people will soon gather round wanting to know all about you and your exciting life, the scoops you have covered, the famous people you have met and any tips about the latest sleaze.

For, like going on the stage, journalism is seen as a glamour job, a cosy world of parties, perks, adventure and power. It certainly helps explain why more than half of today's arts graduates want to go into the media or PR. Compared with more serious careers such as the Bar, the Church, Medicine, Accountancy and the City, journalism is often dismissed as a trendy pursuit that neatly delays the agonies of having to find 'real work'. That is, until the uninitiated start exploring further.

Their findings are likely to be somewhat different. Creative? Yes. Sociable? Certainly. Versatile? Undoubtedly. Arty? Sometimes. Trendy? It depends what you mean by trendy. Working in the media and PR requires tenacity and hard work. It does have moments of glamour, moments when you can indulge yourself and feel an inner glow of satisfaction about a job well done, but stimulating though they are, these professions require long periods of intense, concentrated effort as well as physical and mental stamina.

Working in the media is not a nine-to-five occupation; it is not beholden to set routines, forward planning or job descriptions. You may not have to wear a suit and brogues or a designer dress, but you may find yourself doing a piece of research, writing a press release or inputting a story at 9pm, instead of relaxing after a nourishing meal or enjoying an evening out with friends. You may be about to go home after covering a serious road crash, when your pager tells you to phone the office at once. There has been a race riot in Wembley and the news desk wants you to get over there and file a story post haste. Then when, somewhat exhausted, you start to change for a dinner date with someone you have been longing to see for days, the pealing tones of the telephone rouse you again and you are asked to cover a motorway accident. Media and PR people live on doses of high-octane adrenalin, enjoy less free time than most, and are utterly devoted to their careers.

So what is it like on a local newspaper, the prelude to many a famous journalistic, broadcasting and PR career? The answer is irreverent, personality-led and industrious. Irreverent because your psyche is bombarded with stories about oddballs who steal loaves of bread off milk-floats and then sell them outside Tesco, or out-of-work artists who paint red post-boxes blue to spare letter-writers from eyestrain and motorists from road-blindness. Personality-led, because the media is a network of individualists all bringing their talents and ambitions to bear on a fast, chameleon-like industry; and industrious because reporters and sub-editors work very hard to produce ever-bigger, brasher and brighter "infotainment-based" newspapers. You do not have to be a doctor of philosophy to work on a local newspaper, but you need flair, enthusiasm, independence and courage.

If you are ambitious, you may move on to national newspapers or into radio and television, where you are used to mingling with politicians, celebrities and decision-makers. You may overhear conversations raw enough to ruffle the pinkest liberal's sensitivities, study 'top secret' documents and go home with no idea of what the next day will bring. The speed of national news-rooms makes you see events such as civil wars, towns hit by tidal waves or rugby players who are too big for their boots as surreal items – crucial one minute, dispensable the next, inflated, pummelled into shape, disgorged on to the production line and then quickly forgotten.

You may be first on the scene of an air crash, or happen to witness the formation of a new political party, or get woken in the night by the first exploding bombs of a Middle East crisis. You are an independent operator; your ethics are your own; you are answerable to no one apart from your newspaper or network; you are sometimes disliked, and often befriended, by those who want something out of you. You need only to show your press card when you want a seat at the cinema or to get into a night-club, and are never happier than when you are on the scent of a story, ready to bring drama into people's lives and an exclusive that will make headlines and add brio to your cuttings book.

Media folk like nothing more than writing and gossiping about their jobs, exploits and *faux pas*, making cynical comments about the world around them and laughing at the quirks of some of those who make the news. They have the wry pleasure of watching actors trying to portray them as hard-bitten socialites in films, plays and television series and often see or hear their own names in articles and broadcasts. Yet, it wasn't long ago that many people's idea of the typical journo was of a scruffy-looking individual who asked a few tricky questions before scurrying off to follow his or her dubious calling.

News can be like modern theatre. Take the news sub-editors' desk on a national newspaper. A major item from Reuters arrives. 'Valparaiso earthquake, 2,000 believed dead.' Within seconds, the chief sub-editor and his colleagues will be striving to find a type-face bold and dramatic enough for a front-page splash. The sub-editors will be picking up the first rushes of copy from local correspondents and agencies on their computers and making contact with the paper's picture desk and wire agencies to get big-impact photographs. As the story unfolds, the subs will be constantly urging the foreign and home correspondents to supply more facts with better angles than their rival papers and the event's tragic implications are quickly forgotten in the scramble to produce a professional product. Perhaps this is why commentators refer to the media as a mad, infectious and irresistible business.

CHAPTER ONE

Print Journalism

HOW TO GET INTO PRINT JOURNALISM

A typical conversation between a couple of regulars in the Ox and Ploughshare pub might go something like this: 'Hi James, fancy a pint? By the way have you heard the latest about the flying saucer seen over Farmer Jenkins's land?' 'Yes please. No, my *Sunbury Mail* was delivered late today, so I didn't manage to read anything.' 'It's alright, I've got a copy here. Apparently the local UFO society chairman says it's the third sighting this year.'

Such banter proves the British are unrepentant news addicts. Whereas the Japanese tend to chant before they start work, the British read a newspaper – whether over the breakfast table, on the train, bus or tube, or in the back of a chauffeur-driven limousine. We in Britain produce more national newspapers than any other country, even exceeding the United States, most of whose papers are circulated statewide rather than nationwide. Recent opinion poll statistics show that 65 per cent of the British public reads a paper at some stage of the day and an even bigger 75 per cent on Sundays.

Making that first move

If you want to become a print journalist, you have chosen a rewarding and dedicated career. Like all vocations, there are those who wish to become journalists from a very young age. Others may have opted for the profession because their father, mother or a close relative is a journalist, or they were encouraged by a careers adviser or personal friend. The reasons people choose careers are sometimes unpredictable. A school-friend of mine was pondering his future in the bath during his final term when he decided to throw up a piece of soap. If it came down with the logo facing upwards, he would train to be a doctor. If the reverse happened, he would opt for accountancy. The verdict was medicine, and he has never regretted a moment of it. So what about you? Maybe you were inspired by an article you read or perhaps you have a bit of a deft touch for writing letters or school essays.

Whatever your source of inspiration, working in journalism certainly has a dashing allure. Perhaps you are in the middle of your Finals at college or university and need a job to go to when you leave; perhaps you are frustrated or fed up with your existing job and want something a little more challenging; or maybe you are about to take your A levels and would like to start work instead of going to university. You may be one of those 'Undecideds' that political pollsters are always talking about and need a little encouragement and persuasion.

So here are a few helpful tips. If you are considering a career in journalism, you need to be a bit of an extrovert. You certainly need to enjoy meeting people. You should also be the type of person who does not yearn for a regular nine-to-five existence, for journalists often work unusual hours – it is part of the job's vocational nature. However, as those hours are apt to be interesting and diverting, it is not exactly an onerous burden.

Let us now look at some of the more specific qualities needed to be a print journalist – in other words, a reporter on a newspaper or magazine.

Persistence and dedication

Reporters talk to a large number of people, make incessant phone calls and visit a wide variety of individuals, institutions and groups during their working day. This often involves having to extract a sizeable amount of information from your sources – sometimes after several other avenues have failed. This needs persistence. You may have heard of the famous occasion when the broadcaster and journalist Jeremy Paxman asked Conservative Home Secretary Michael Howard the same question 14 times on BBC's *Newsnight*, as he sought to get an answer about a political issue. He may have failed, but it was not for want of trying – and he won an award for his persistence.

Sometimes reporters have to work awkward hours. You may, for instance, have to cover a fire on a lazy Sunday afternoon or carry on working at the office until late into the evening. This needs dedication. So you need to be enthusiastic about the job and to see it more as a way of life than a nine-to-five occupation. It is not such a tall order. There are many other more mundane careers where you have to put in extra work, sometimes for scant reward.

Resilience

Being a reporter is fun. Basically you are getting paid for something you enjoy. There is nothing to compare with the adrenalin of following up a really good story, especially if it ends up as an exclusive, with a big by-line. Yes, reporting can really get the adrenalin going. There are times when you have to face tragedy and the aftermath of accidents. Because reporting is your job, you cope with these situations. Sometimes people get a bit of a kick out of being rude or cheeky to the press. This too is part of the job. You cannot expect roses all the way, and you must accept any surly remarks with a ready smile. Just as a computer salesman's job is to sell equipment, yours is to get a story, so anything that distracts you from your purpose is irrelevant. The fun and adrenalin more than make up for it.

Diplomacy, tact and humour

A reporter deals with a huge cross-section of people. Some are mad, some bad, others charming. Be tactful and considerate when you are talking to people. They won't like it if you are terse or abrupt like the Hollywood image of the hard-nosed reporter with the brusque, uncaring manner. Anyway, it is far more rewarding to be nice to people, even if you are chasing a big story! So be conversational and good-humoured with a light touch, when talking to contacts and members of the public. Even the most pompous popinjays like a bit of banter, and humour always lightens the conversation. It can also be a useful tactic when, later in your career, you are trying to extract important information from people. Humour disarms people and makes them more likely to open up to you. It also shows you don't take yourself too seriously. Sometimes news is so bizarre and entertaining that it will provide you with an endless source of stories to share with your colleagues or mates at the local pub.

Curiosity

Reporters need to be curious – a polite way of saying 'nosy'. You certainly need to have a healthy interest in current affairs and in what is going on around you. The Hollywood columnist and wit Dorothy Parker said:

'Four be the things I'd been better without
Love, curiosity, freckles and doubt.'

Love and doubt are certainly not keys to journalistic success. Curiosity (and probably freckles) are. Without inquisitiveness, Dorothy Parker wouldn't have been the journalist she was. You must always be asking questions and trying to find answers. That's what reporting is all about and asking the question 'why' is an invaluable reporting ploy during a lull in a long interview.

Healthy scepticism

A reporter needs some healthy scepticism. You will hear news stories from a myriad of sources: reputable agencies, members of the public, your own contacts, friends. Though most of them will be authentic, especially if they are a 'usually reliable source', the occasional one will not. Always check and double check your sources, particularly if you have any misgivings.

Hoaxers can make a lot of money from gullible newspapers. The most notorious was a man named Jo Flynn, who had at least six different aliases and disguises until he was jailed for 20 years for fraud. His hoaxing career brought him an average of £100,000 a year from national newspapers, TV stations and magazines for his 'news stories' about everything from spies to satellites.

Writing

You need to be able to write clearly and concisely. You do not need the literary flair of an Evelyn Waugh to be a reporter. Writing newspaper reports is a discipline or craft that you will acquire through practice, picking up techniques and favourite phrases that add colour and clarity to your writing as you go along. Read newspapers and magazines to get a feel for the writing styles. There may be journalists you respect. See how they put their ideas across. Listen to the precise way news bulletins are broadcast, and read books voraciously. It will all add to your armoury as a working reporter.

'Nous'

Reporters need *nous*. If, for instance, you are searching for a phone number and cannot find it in the relevant telephone directory, use your head. If your subject is an actor, try Equity, the actor's union, or *Stage* magazine which keeps a directory of actors' agents. If that fails contact ICM (International Creative Management), Britain's biggest actors' agency, for an answer. If they don't handle the actor, they may well know a company that does.

Nous is knowing the best time to phone contacts – usually around

2.30pm after lunch when they are feeling relaxed and not at 7.30pm or 8.00pm when they may be in the middle of their evening meal. Nous is also knowing when to ask your colleagues questions – not when they are in the middle of a story or facing an impending deadline.

Psychology

As a reporter, you need to have a grasp of what makes people tick. For instance, if you know someone is impatient, don't be too persistent in your questioning. They will start glancing at their watch and say they have another more pressing appointment. Always respect people's views and feelings and listen to what they have to say, even if you would rather be in three other places.

A nose for news

A 'nose for news' is an instinct about what makes a good story. Some are born with it. Others acquire it. Equally important is to know what style of reporting appeals to your readers. For some reason new towns (or relatively new ones) like Harlow, Hemel Hempstead, Welwyn Garden City and Crawley tend to attract a hard, tabloid-style of reporting. Perhaps it is because the residents tend to be young and striving with a clear-cut view of the future. In more traditional towns such as Guildford and Gloucester, newspapers tend to be community-minded, more concerned about what the local people and the council are doing than in exposing corruption in town halls. Occasionally, in smaller towns, you find pioneering editors with real community spirit who write powerful leaders imploring the council to do this or the chamber of commerce to do that. These papers play a valuable role in the community.

An overview

The *Sunday Times* reporter Nicholas Tomalin neatly summed up the qualities needed to be a newspaper reporter in his book, *Stop The Press, I Want To Get On*. He described them as having: 'Rat-like cunning, a plausible manner and a little literary ability'. Not a bad summary!

If you think you have most of the above qualities, then journalism is probably for you. The next step is getting into the profession.

HOW TO BECOME A NEWSPAPER REPORTER

Work experience

Newspaper editors are always impressed by job candidates who have had work experience. It means they have taken the trouble to learn about the job and to know some of its ins and outs. When you are considering how to get into journalism, you couldn't do better than apply to the local papers in your area for work experience. The best time to apply is in the summer, when staff reporters take their holidays. If accepted, you will usually be taken on for two weeks – with a proviso that if all goes well, you may be given a slightly longer period or perhaps another spell on the newspaper. If, when you apply, you have already done some journalism on school or college newspapers, that will help your application.

The merits of work experience

Working on placement is the best way to familiarise yourself with the job of reporter. You will 'shadow' reporters on assignments such as court stories, accidents and local events, and they may ask you to write up the story yourself, so you can compare notes. A lot of would-be journalists get their first by-lines (signed articles) while on placement. You may be asked to re-write company press releases (publicity information supplied by organisations) in the style of the newspaper. Another favourite is to cover an amateur drama production. These can be fun and give you a chance to express yourself. You also get your name at the bottom of the article. You may also be asked to produce ideas for feature articles. These are more in-depth than news stories and are usually about interesting local organisations or issues.

Work experience is the best mirror you can have for what working in journalism is all about. It will also tell you whether journalism is for you. Your next step is to get some training.

Applying for courses

There are three main training options for those who want to get into the industry. The first is the NCE (National Certificate Examination) run by the National Council for the Training of Journalists (NCTJ). This involves going on a 12-month or 20-week pre-entry course (depending on your qualifications) at a college or university, followed by 18 months on a local newspaper. The second is the National Vocational Qualification or NVQ. This is also taken at a college, but involves a quota of work experience, the idea being to include written articles in a course portfolio. The third method of entry is to join a local newspaper that usually has its own training scheme.

The NCE

The NCE, formerly the Proficiency Test, gives trainees a thorough grounding in Local Government, Central Government, Shorthand, Newspaper Practice, Law and Ethics. This is usually done on a full-time basis with frequent tests and lectures given by experts in the field. Candidates can also expect to do a short spell of work experience. Those with degrees go on a 20-week, fast-track course; while those with two (and in some cases one) A-levels join a one-year pre-entry course. At the end, both take preliminary tests in their subjects of study plus 100wpm shorthand. With the college's help, they can then apply for a job as a trainee on an NCTJ-approved local newspaper. This lasts for 18 months and usually involves a six-month trial. At the end of the period, trainees take the NCE examination.

If they pass, they can call themselves fully-fledged journalists. One of the most successful NCE centres is Highbury College, Portsmouth where more than 80 per cent of students regularly get jobs before the end of the 20-week course for a signing-on fee of £1,300, including exam fees, books, guest speakers and trips to law courts.

Some useful alternatives: Bournemouth and Sheffield Universities and the University of Central Lancashire run three-year journalism degree courses (including work experience) approved by the NCTJ. This is a recognised alternative training route to the NCE. City University, which used to be NCTJ-backed, has a one-year journalism diploma for postgraduates or anyone with seven years journalism experience. Many City University-trained journalists go on to regional or national newspapers.

The best way to find out about approved courses is to contact the NCTJ (*see* Glossary, p. 161).

The NVQ

Newspaper journalism NVQs began in 1992 as part of a government drive to get people back to work by matching them to jobs. The NVQ has two main merits. The first is that it is hands-on, which makes it an ideal match for journalism's practical nature. The second is that it is based on a student's collection of published articles. This means it is not examination-based. Some people have an examination mentality – a talent for producing the goods on the day. This can be unfair on those who don't. An aptitude for journalism is best judged over a longish period, not necessarily two days of examinations. Sometimes those who do not have an exam mentality have far greater journalistic aptitude than those who do. This makes the NVQ a much-lauded method of training.

Like those taking the NCE, students of the NVQ study government, shorthand, law and ethics. At the same time, they produce a thorough portfolio of their work, most of which is carried during periods of work experience on local newspapers. The NVQ, which like the NCE is approved by the NCTJ, is mainly run by colleges and universities, although some newspapers also have their own courses.

The periods of placement range from about six weeks to three or four months. This gives students enough time to learn all about reporting on newspapers. During the year, their work is continually assessed by journalist-lecturers, ending with a full scrutiny by a verifier from the Royal Society of Arts (RSA), sponsor of the NVQ. Students also take shorthand tests up to 100wpm. When they have finished their portfolios and gained 100wpm shorthand, students receive their NVQ diploma (it has a degree status). The study period is from one to three years, so a candidate who is working part-time is able to finish the course. Many NVQ students are offered jobs while working on placement.

Direct entry

The third way of getting into journalism is to apply directly to a local or regional newspaper. If you have already done some work experience or written for school or college magazines, editors will be more likely to take you on. You will then receive all your training on the job. Many newspapers run the NCE, the NVQ and their own group diploma. Trainees will be sent for either 12-weeks' block release or one-day-a-week at a journalism training college, at the end of which they will take an examination or produce a portfolio, and thus qualify in the same way as a pre-entry candidate. In a way, this is probably the best training method for journalism, if you manage to obtain a job. For you are both employed and trained at the same time. The way to apply is to get a list of local newspapers from

Willing's Press Guide or *Benn's Media Directory* at your local library, then sit down, write a smart letter of introduction and send it off together with your CV to as many newspapers as you can. It may mean moving to another part of the country, but it will prove a career move par excellence.

Am I too old to get into journalism?

There is no real age barrier to a journalism career. You may be a very young 50-year-old who doesn't mind working with younger people and many newspapers are staffed by older, more experienced reporters. Sometimes editors make it their policy to take on trainees in their 30s and 40s who have worked in other fields. Richard Parsons, editor-in-chief of the *Surrey Herald* series in Chertsey, took on to his staff a former market gardener and a building contracts manager – both of whom were studying on a local journalism NVQ in their 30s – instead of a long list of young hopefuls. He did this 'because they had nous and experience of people and industry which I knew would add depth and knowledge to the way they reported stories – both reporters have been a great success'.

Other ways to learn the job

Many London and provincial colleges and universities run one-year foundation courses in journalism, including one for those in the 25–35 age group. These are usually taken in the evening and give aspiring journalists a chance to be taught by working journalists about the media; the history of national and regional newspapers and how they are run; and to practise their reporting skills on life-like assignments.

Case study

Malcolm Prescott became editor of the *Surrey Comet and Guardian* series at the age of 27. He had wanted to be a reporter from the age of 14. He left Tiffin grammar school in Kingston, Surrey, with three A levels in 1987, when there were no journalism degrees, so he decided to join the pre-entry course at Highbury College, Portsmouth. During his training Malcolm spent six weeks on *The News*, Portsmouth, then just before the end he applied to the *Surrey Comet* and was offered a job as a trainee. He took to the job immediately and was promoted to chief reporter within a year, even though he was still technically a trainee. After passing the NCE, he spent a year in the USA, Australia and the Far East, paying his way with news items and articles he picked up on his travels. He returned to Britain after 'three blissful months on a Bangkok beach' and was offered a job as news editor of the *Surrey Herald* newspaper, later joining the *Comet and Guardian* as news editor, assistant editor and finally editor.

Secrets of Malcolm's success

Malcolm says he had the advantage of knowing the area where he worked, as he had lived in mid-Surrey all his life. He knew the local haunts and meeting places, as well as many of the area's personalities. This provided him with a rich fund of local news stories which was recognised and appreciated by the seniors on the newspapers where he worked, and contributed to his rapid promotion on the two Surrey newspapers. He continues to do a considerable amount of freelance work for magazines and newspapers – mostly from stories he has picked up in the local community. This is, he says, what makes journalism such a special job for him.

Advice to trainees

Malcolm cannot praise work experience highly enough. 'Journalism is a job for individuals and they need the opportunity to develop their talents in the workplace, so they can see the "fruits of their labours" when the newspaper comes out,' he says. He emphasises that it is very important for reporters to develop interests in fields other than news, such as sport, theatre, music, television and general entertainment. This will give them greater scope when they look for jobs, particularly with the huge range of interests now covered by newspapers and magazines. The national tabloids in particular have large entertainment sections employing their own teams of reporters.

HOW DO I BECOME A MAGAZINE JOURNALIST?

What are glossy, stylish and eye-catching and take up most of the space on news-stands? The answer: magazines. Magazines are mainly for leisure- and spare-time reading. They enable the reader to ponder, digest and fantasise about the chic culottes the in-crowd are fond of wearing or that shiny, cosmic-looking car that would look sassy on your terraced forecourt. From 6,000 magazines ten years ago to more than 10,000 today – the bursting cascade of magazines, house journals and newsletters speak for themselves. Think of almost any pastime or specialist subject – from golf to herbal medicine – and there is a good chance there is a magazine or journal that caters for it.

How do I get on to a magazine?

There are a number of proven routes to a magazine job. The good news is that it is easier than it was. This is because newspapers and magazines have become closer in format. Most national newspapers have separate magazine-style sections, and the journalists who work for one sector often write for the other as well.

Work experience

As with local newspapers, a lot of magazine editors take people for two weeks' work experience. Again, the best time to apply is the summer. If you have a specialised interest, such as cooking or handicrafts, this may help your application. When you arrive, you will assist with photo-shoots of fashions, products and people, write occasional picture captions, help research articles, compose letters, and carry out more mundane tasks such as filing and inputting people's copy. If the period goes well, it may be extended, you may be entrusted with a short article or two, and it is not unknown for people with something useful to offer to gain jobs while on work experience. A spell on a magazine will certainly give you the edge over job candidates who have not been near one.

Training courses

The one-year postgraduate diploma in magazine journalism, approved by the Periodical Training Council (PTC), is probably the industry favourite. Two of the most successful venues for this course, which covers reporting, feature-writing, interviewing, law, sub-editing and shorthand, are London's City University and Cardiff's University of Wales. Other PTC-backed courses are Bournemouth University's three-year degree in multi-media jour-nalism, which costs only £1,000; London's Westminster University one-year diploma in magazine journalism for ethnic minorities; and the one-year course at Highbury College, Portsmouth, which is open to both graduates and non-graduates. Two highly recommended courses for non-graduates are the London College of Printing's one-year diploma for students with one A-level and four GCSE passes, including English; and the London College of Fashion's three-year degree in fashion journalism, design and promotion.

Some colleges run shorter courses for magazine hopefuls. The London College of Printing holds evening classes for people with specialist skills who wish to become journalists and 13-week courses for those who already have BTEC diplomas or technical qualifications; PMA Training in Cambridge runs a nine-week magazine course for graduates; and the PTC runs short courses on different aspects of magazine work.

For students who are working full- or part-time, the NCTJ has a three- to six-month distance learning course for would-be magazine journalists. Students pay a total of £415, work from home and take ten modules covering writing, collecting news and feature stories, sub-editing, layout and media law. To obtain a full list of magazine courses, contact the Periodical Publishers Association (*see* Glossary, p. 161) for their *Magazines Training Directory* and 'A Career in Magazines' booklet which has a useful directory of magazine companies to approach.

The large magazine groups, EMAP, IPC Magazines, Conde-Nast, Reed Business Information, Future Publishing, Miller Freeman and Reader's Digest run their own in-house training courses for new employees. Trainees usually work on two or three different periodicals in the same group, gaining keyboarding skills as well as specialist knowledge, before settling on one of them. You can also apply to some magazines for short, vocational courses, followed by spells of work experience.

The NVQ

Like their newspaper counterparts, magazine entrants can take an NVQ in journalism sponsored by the PTC and the Royal Society of Arts. Candidates can choose either sub-editing or writing for this hands-on qualification and combine several spells working on magazines with a college course run by professional journalists. This vocational qualification takes from one to three years, depending on the trainee's commitments, and is based on putting together a portfolio of published work that is continuously monitored by journalist-tutors. Back at college, the student studies law, public affairs and journalistic techniques and, on the writing NVQ, shorthand up to 100wpm. He or she also attends lectures on all aspects of magazine work. At the end of the course, the student's portfolio is given a final scrutiny by a visiting RSA verifier. If successful, the student is awarded the Periodical Journalism NVQ which is the equivalent of a college degree.

Applying for that first job

There are several useful pointers to bear in mind when applying for a job on a magazine. First, a magazine degree, diploma or NVQ obviously holds sway, particularly if you have also done work experience. However, if you don't have a relevant qualification, employers like to see some evidence of your work, such as school or college magazine articles or newsletters you may have written. If you are applying to a specialist magazine, a relevant degree would be an asset; while, if you are a practising doctor, lawyer, chemist, scientist or in a host of other professions, there is a growing number of specialist magazines and trade journals ready to employ your inside knowledge and experience as a journalist.

Most new entrants start as editorial assistants, helping to research articles, organise photographic sessions and write captions and news items. You may well be asked to carry out more routine tasks such as letter-writing and filing. However, progress is rapid and, if all goes well, it won't be long before you are writing your own signed articles. Another good method-of-entry is to start off as a secretary or administrative assistant. That way you will be able to try out your ideas and maybe write an article or two, which may eventually lead to a staff writing post.

If you are passionate about working in magazines, there is no better way than to send in articles on your favourite topics or interests. That way, the section editors will get to know you, and you to know them. The secrets of success are market research (see pp. 34–37) and determination; and, as the majority of magazine articles are written by freelances, you stand as good a chance of getting one of yours published as the next person.

To find a list of magazines and trade journals, the latest editions of *Benn's UK Media Directory*, the *Writers' & Artists' Yearbook* and *Willing's Press Guide* at your local library all carry informative guides with addresses and telephone numbers.

CHAPTER TWO

Freelance Journalism

A thirty-year-old skin-diver called Jill Neville manages to elude the jaws of a shark in a small lagoon and is swept out to sea by a swirling current. She clings to her tiny, 18-inch-long diving float for two days and nights before being dumped by the tide on the shore of a tropical island. A few hours later she is spotted and rescued by a passing helicopter. This story was told by Mrs Neville in *Reader's Digest*. It is a gripping one. But getting such a story published is within the scope of many people with little more than a smattering of writing experience.

That is the magic of freelance journalism. It enables you to write about your experiences, ideas, job or interests and get paid for them as well. You do not need the short-story telling talent of a Somerset Maugham, just a reasonable grasp of the English language and enough initiative to know which magazines to contact. You might be a keen angler writing about the monster that got away; you may have been inspired by a bizarre holiday, or perhaps you have written 1,500 words about a rare type of rock. Nearly every interest, hobby or job has a freelance market – and what makes it saleable is your personal experience of it.

However, to make a regular living out of writing needs technique. You must have a grasp of such priorities as the right market to aim for, the style of writing, and, very important, how to approach editors. All this takes practice. It may be a few months before you get your first item published, but after that it can be all unexpurgated pleasure! There are some freelance journalists, like Alan Coren, Claire Rayner and Miles Kington, who have become famous for their contributions to newspapers and magazines. There are others who are well-known for writing about one specialist subject such as law, science or sport. Whatever category you fit into, there is no doubt you can make a good second living out of freelance writing.

Finding the spark
You may become a freelance by chance. A new magazine catches

your eye in your local newsagent. It has bright ideas and echoes many of your views; its editor is looking for new talent. So you contact them with an idea. Another scenario may be that a work colleague asks you to contribute a 'piece' on a subject you know about for the company's house journal. Or perhaps you see a short story competition advertised, and open a letter three months later to find that your entry has been shortlisted for inclusion in a book. Freelance journalism is a career of many possibilities!

One way to test your mettle is to join an evening course in freelance writing or journalism at a further education or adult college. Here you will be able to listen to and work with a lecturer who has experience in the field. He or she will ask you to carry out writing assignments, which often unearth the writer within. With their varying interests, ideas and occupations, your course colleagues will often be a source of stimulation too. Maybe, after some success in selling articles, you will decide to consider freelancing as a serious career option – though you are sensible enough not to give up your day job until you have become established.

Getting a letter published

Many freelances begin by writing letters to local newspapers. Weekly correspondence about the siting of a new indoor swimming pool, a noisy nightclub, or a petition to keep open a local railway station always make for lively copy. If you are feeling particularly bold, you could write a persuasive letter to a national newspaper or magazine. It is very satisfying to see your name in the *Independent* or *Daily Telegraph* letters pages.

Writing competitions

The joy of freelancing is that as your confidence grows, so will your success. After getting some letters published, you could branch out into magazines, looking out for competitions or short story opportunities and getting the flavour by reading other people's stories and how they write about different subjects.

One young freelance I know went on a postal writing course. After a couple of months he started writing letters to his local newspaper. One memorable Tuesday, he had one published about the need for cycle lanes on a particularly busy highway in his local town. This boosted his confidence and soon two more of his letters were published. Then one day while looking through a copy of *Bella* magazine, he saw an article-writing competition about 'The Day I

Met My Partner'. He entered and to his delight won first prize and a sizeable sum of money. Yet, apart from a couple of school essays, our friend had never done any writing before.

Going the whole hog!

If you are taken by the freelancing bug, it is obviously better not to leave your present job until you are confident of bringing in a respectable income. One good way to do this is to find a subject or niche that interests you and which your work seems to fit neatly into. Build up a file of articles you have researched and possibly had published as well as responses and comments by editors to your work, then when you have a regular stream of work coming in, with one or two big contracts to help pay the mortgage, take the plunge.

What qualities do I need?

Going solo

As a fully-fledged freelance you must enjoy your own company – you are on your own for long periods and must often forego the friendship and camaraderie of work colleagues around you.

Patience is a virtue

You must be patient and resourceful, trying every market until you get a result. Be prepared to wait three months for some of your pay cheques, though not prepared to wait any longer! Doggedness is a virtue. If something goes wrong it is you, and you alone, who has to take the responsibility. You don't have editors or colleagues to fall back on.

Self-discipline

You must have self-discipline. If you want to spend the afternoon at an art gallery or dance the night away with some high-spirited friends, you can do so without a few sharp words from your boss for turning up late the next day. If you suddenly want to take a two-week break in the Azores you do not have to get anyone's permission. Just go and enjoy – and make sure you put in some extra hours when you get back! However, you must try and be healthy and take your holidays or breaks at sensible times; for, as a self-employed person, you do not have the comfort of a regular monthly salary with paid holiday and sickness leave.

How do I start?

Strategy

First you must regard yourself as the owner of a small business. You must have a strategy about who you are selling your articles to, how often you need to sell them and what sort of cash flow you need to pay the mortgage each month.

Some people form a limited company with their partner or accountant as company secretary. This means you are not liable for any debts, should your freelancing fail to work out. You certainly need to register yourself with your local tax district as a self-employed person and pay a regular National Insurance stamp for your future pension. As a self-employed person, you will be able to offset overheads such as lighting, heating and telephone bills, travel, car petrol, office furnishings, stationery, and working lunches against tax.

Cash

You will need money in the bank to start you off. If you don't have savings or private money, negotiate an overdraft facility of at least £3,000 to £4,000 with your bank manager, after presenting him with a business plan drawn up by your accountant. You never know when lean months may occur or when payments may be delayed or late for some reason.

Accountant

Get a street-wise and preferably local accountant who can get to know all about you and your freelance work. Don't go to a large city firm that will not be able to offer the same personal service as a smaller one and will send you large annual invoices. A reliable solicitor will also be an asset over copyright matters for your articles, possible libel cases, and the 'small print' in contracts.

Office

Get a comfortable and quiet working base. This may be your own study, a small office in a nearby town or village, or perhaps shared accommodation with other freelances or businesses. You need enough space for a desk, telephone(s), computer, fax and filing system. Make sure it's easily accessible and warm.

Get equipped

Equip yourself with good working aids, including:

- good quality headed notepaper and business cards;
- a comfortable desk and chair, plus two more for visitors;
- a good personal computer (it's difficult to go wrong with an AppleMac), with e-mail and internet, printer and fax machine;
- a filing cabinet and shelving for books and accessories.

Organisation

Some thrive on routine; others prefer to adopt a more flexible approach. It would certainly benefit you at the start of your freelance career to go to work at the same time every day – say at 9am and then finish at 5pm or so. You will soon develop your own working pace and rhythm, much of which will be based on the timing of your article deadlines and the size of your workload. In time you may prefer to start later in the morning when commissioning editors are just sipping their first cup of coffee and going through the day's post and then carrying on into the evening!

It is most unlikely you'll finish at the same time every day. You may have a deadline drawing ominously close or some new commissions that take you into the ember hours. Evenings can be a most productive time for writing, with the added bonus of no intrusive phone calls or faxes filtering through.

Reading matter

Make sure you receive a regular daily supply of newspapers and magazines and listen to the early morning news, such as Radio Four's *Today* programme. This will keep you abreast of current affairs and provide you with ideas for articles.

Notebooks

Keep a notebook, so that you can jot down ideas as and when you think of them. You will also need to keep copies of interviews and research notes for articles in case you need to refer back to them or write an article at a later date. Someone may query a quotation you may have used in an article. By keeping copies of your notebooks, you can refer back to these.

Records

Keep a working record of all the editors you speak to and what was said on the phone, plus copies of all correspondence.

Also, keep copies of articles and information you collect while researching. You may need to refer to these. They will also be invaluable for new ideas.

You will almost certainly have your own cuttings file by now. Make sure this is smartly presented, with publications and dates clearly written next to the articles. Editors and prospective clients are sure to want to see these from time to time.

Marketing and presentation

It is very important that people get to know about you, if your reputation hasn't already sailed before you! Quite simply, you must market yourself, and you can do this in a number of ways:

1. Use business cards whenever you meet new contacts or acquaintances. You never know when someone may need your services.

2. The telephone, e-mail and fax are very effective marketing tools. You may already have targeted a number of magazines you wish to write for. A timely telephone call to a commissioning editor who may just be looking for an article on your chosen subject could prove a winner. Buy a web-site to sell your wares. You never know when someone will spot you mid-surf. Even if it brings you in only one commission a year, it will more than pay for itself.

3. Use *Press Gazette*, the journalists' weekly newspaper, to advertise yourself. Why not speak to the chief reporter Jean Morgan and see if she will do a write-up about your new enterprise and what you have to offer newspapers and magazines?

An insertion in the *Freelance Directory* is a must. It is published annually and is a commissioning editor's reference book, especially when they are looking for new names and talent. Strategically-placed advertisements highlighting your areas of interest – such as, say, Far East travel or the history of landmines – in *The Journalist* (the newspaper of the National Union of Journalists), and in the *Media Guardian*, which comes out on Mondays and is read by key media folk, could pay dividends. Take advantage of any advertising offers (such as big discounts) you come across, too.

4. It's important to have smart-looking stationery bearing your name, interests and logo, plus phone, fax, e-mail and web-site numbers.

5. Send query letters and faxes to magazines, remembering to follow them up afterwards. (It is so easy for an editor to put your correspondence on a growing pile of mail and forget about it.)

6. Another good way to market yourself is to send personal leaflets advertising your wares to companies or organisations you intend to write about. They may be looking for someone to write a brochure, a series of press releases, or to edit a newsletter. Your piece of salesmanship may just nudge the task in your direction. A telephone call or fax to a series of companies could also lead to work, and will make a comparatively small dent in your telephone bill. Another way to attract work from companies is to place advertisements in their trade journals.

7. Always take the newspapers, magazines and trade journals of your chosen specialist field, so you are up-to-date with ideas and activities.

8. Look out for advertisements from companies or individuals in different publications who may need the services of a freelance journalist. You could even put up a card in your local newsagents.

9. Join the freelance branch of the NUJ and attend their meetings. This will provide valuable networking with other freelances and keep you informed about the industry. The NUJ can also be a most fruitful source of advice for budding freelances.

10. Go on courses – sub-editing, QuarkXpress and feature-writing, and any refresher course you may come across. These are often advertised in the back of *Press Gazette*. This will also be a valuable source of marketing and networking, where you can meet other freelances and journalist-lecturers and bounce ideas off one another.

A valuable tip
Be shrewd with your marketing. Take advantage of as many cut-price offers as you can, and always try to weigh up the benefits against the costs. Just occasionally, go out on a limb. Remember that famous business school line: 'You have to speculate to accumulate.' If an advertisement opportunity works and brings you in commissions, repeat it. The longer you are established, the more recommendations you will get as more and more people get to know you as a journalist par excellence!

Alternative niches
Sub-editing
This is one of the most fruitful fields for freelancing (*see* also Chapter 9). If the idea of newspaper and magazine production and

editing appeals to you, it is a creative and stimulating sector with considerable earning potential.

As technology becomes more streamlined and newspapers and magazines get larger, more style-conscious and designer-led, the importance of the sub-editor or production person continues to grow. Employers are always on the lookout for journalists with computer inputting and sub-editing skills. A quick glance in the recruitment sections of *Press Gazette* or Monday's *Media Guardian* will show the number of advertisements for journalists with QuarkXpress skills.

One of the main reasons employers like taking on casual labour is that it is cheaper than using permanent staff. They can pay an hourly rate and do not have to subsidise sickness, insurance and holidays. The remuneration for casual subbing work can be high; you can expect to be paid £100 plus a day on most publications, and you can do your own freelance writing at the same time. Here is a guide to subbing rates (for daily shifts) on a number of publications:

Mail on Sunday: £140
Nature: £140
Travel Trade Gazette: £120
Observer: £140
Sunday Times: £120
Daily Telegraph: £100
Daily Mail: £100
Doctor: £110
Parenting: £95
Top Sante: £95
Parking Review: £75
Average local newspaper £70–£80

If you are not a trained journalist, don't worry. There are a number of intensive sub-editing and computer inputting courses you could go on. The NCTJ run several; others are advertised in *Press Gazette*. When you have completed a course, why not telephone a number of magazines and newspapers that appeal to you and ask if you can do some casual subbing shifts. They will normally give you a paid two-day try-out, and if that is satisfactory, offer you more work. It may eventually lead to a full- or part-time job if you want it. It could certainly lead to regular shifts. If the direct marketing approach doesn't appeal to you, there are a number of sub-editing agencies, most of whom advertise in *Press Gazette*, that will get work for you.

If you are interested in newspaper subbing, it helps to have done some reporting beforehand, as this teaches you the mechanics of getting stories and articles. You also need to have media law knowledge and to know the 'ins and outs' of libel, court cases and copyright. *Essential Law for Journalists* by Greenwood and Welch (available from the NCTJ) covers all this clearly and concisely. On magazines, you rarely need prior reporting experience, just a feeling for good writing!

On some publications, subs are more important than writers. They re-write stories, and occasionally even write them, adding headlines, captions and standfirsts (*see* Chapter 9, pp. 124–130) and often designing pages which make full use of their inputting resources. Though more desk-bound than reporters, subs are certainly as creative and experience the same adrenalin when deadlines approach.

Reporting and writing shifts

If you have done reporting or writing before, you can use your freelancing talents to do writing shifts on magazines and trade journals. As for sub-editing shifts, you need to go to their offices to do this and cover stories just like a normal staff member of the publication. They will give you a try-out for the first two days. If all goes well, they will ask you in for more work. The way to get these shifts is to telephone magazines or journals that appeal to you and ask them for shift-work, mentioning of course that you are a freelance and have previous experience. The advantage of casual work is that it will fit round your other freelance work and help supplement your income. You could do this on more than one publication, too.

Another opportunity is to apply for reporting shifts on newspapers. Some local papers use freelances to supplement their staffing levels, especially when reporters are on holiday in the summer months. The nationals also employ casual reporters, and if you are an ambitious, newly-trained journalist this is a good way to get noticed and land a job on a big newspaper. Again the summer is the best time to apply.

Here are a few examples of day-shift rates:

Inside Housing: £115
Supermarketing: £120
National newspapers: £100-£140
Average local newspaper: £80

Writing brochures and press releases

Should you depend on your partner for your main source of income – or even if you don't – you could get a part-time job in the press office of a small company or charity, helping to write pamphlets, brochures or press releases (information sent to the press about an organisation's activities). In this way, you can concentrate on your article-writing the rest of the time.

Working as a specialist

There are a large range of house journals and newspaper columns catering for doctors, lawyers and financial experts, and some of them write as well as practise. Look how often you see columns headed: 'A Doctor Writes...' There is also considerable scope for computer personnel, health and fitness specialists, gardeners and cooks. So if you are a specialist, there are many publications that would be interested in your work. One important point: if you are writing about a specialist interest or job, it is often a good idea to have a back-up subject as well. It means that if the market for one diminishes, you can concentrate on the other, and vice versa (*see* Chapter 3, pp. 28–34).

Book and technical-writing

One sector worth considering is book- or booklet-writing. Many companies need competent freelance writers to put together technical guides and booklets (computer handbooks are very popular). Either look out for advertisements, or approach companies and offer your services. There are also professional book-writing companies who use freelances for writing or proof-reading manuscripts.

Public relations

This is one of the media's burgeoning sectors. Companies always need skilled people to help produce press handouts or organise exhibitions. You will need training (*see* Chapter 5, pp. 70–75) beforehand. Then, why not set yourself up as a PR consultant, working from home, perhaps with some desktop publishing back-up. Using a lethal combination of QuarkXpress and Photoshop, you will be able to produce high-quality glossy colour brochures, thus saving you money and sub-contracting time. A lot of ex-journalists opt for this freelance route.

Should I go full-time or part-time?

If you decide to become a part-time freelance journalist, you are taking a brave and exciting step, with the satisfaction of writing articles about favourite topics or interests and the kudos of seeing them in print afterwards.

If, after reading this, you decide to become a full-time freelance journalist, give yourself ample time to build up to decision day. Keep sending in articles in your spare-time and give editors the opportunity to get to know your work. A commissioning editor may well start asking **you** for work after you have placed a couple of your articles! When you have two or three such editors on your books, regular commissions and the prospects of a regular income poised on the horizon, you can consider making it a full-time career. Now is the time to approach a local accountant and make a business plan.

Trained journalists

You may already be a trained journalist who wishes to go out on your own due to redundancy; a wish to write for more than one publication; the convenience of working from home (perhaps you are a mother or father with young children to care for); or for several other plausible reasons. You will almost certainly have found a niche or area you like working in, in which case going freelance will be an extension of that. Having worked as a journalist will give you the confidence to handle most things, whether reporting, subbing, PR, writing press releases, feature-writing or promoting products. When you have acquired a bit of a name for yourself, your negotiating skills and pay cheques will be considerably boosted. Even better, you could hire an agent to do this for you.

Case Study

Rhondda Cox is an American-born freelance journalist and copywriter. After taking a two-year marketing diploma, she joined a radio station in Denver, Colorado, selling air-time to advertisers. Though most of her time was spent negotiating with clients over the telephone, she also did some copywriting (writing commercials) for smaller advertisers. After eight successful years in which she became the state's leading air-time sales executive, Rhondda decided to spend two years travelling. She went to Europe, including a year learning French in Geneva, before reaching England. She was offered a job as manager of a ski supplier where part of her duties was to write the copy in the company's catalogues. The company grew from three to 30 employees and she was made a director.

However, Rhondda found her new post too administration-based, so she left to become a freelance copywriter. She also joined a one-year access course in journalism and creative writing at a local adult college, so enjoying the course that she decided to try selling articles as well as copywriting. After a couple of months, she managed to get two health articles accepted by a small local magazine. Then she had a lucky break. She saw a series of articles in the *Daily Mail* about unusual reunions with loved ones. She had just had a highly successful reunion in Amsterdam with her father whom she hadn't seen for 20 years. It fitted the bill perfectly, so Rhondda approached the section editor who asked her to send in a synopsis. Then she telephoned Rhondda and asked her to send 800 words. On receiving the article, the editor immediately phoned her back saying they were going to publish it and could she send in a photograph.

The account appeared in the *Daily Mail's Weekend* section three weeks later. Rhondda says: 'It was the piece of luck I needed and I realised that if I could write for the *Daily Mail*, I could write for anyone.' Rhondda decided to concentrate on writing articles about her two main interests – skiing and travel. More and more of them were published until she was able to successfully combine two careers – freelance journalism and copywriting. 'The work goes in cycles. When I have a lot of copywriting work, I do less journalism, and vice versa. They balance each other up very nicely,' she says.

Rhondda's advice to budding freelances

While she was writing articles, Rhondda developed an interest in photography which became another source of income. She advises other freelances to do the same. 'Most subjects lend themselves to photographs, and more and more magazines and newspapers are relying on freelances to send in photographs or illustrations with their articles, thus saving them having to use staff people. You will receive a good fee for these – sometimes it has doubled my article fee.'

She says the secret of her success as a freelance is boldness. 'Don't be afraid to telephone commissioning editors cold. You have nothing to lose. It is not always easy to get commissions at first, so don't be afraid of rejection and it may take many telephone calls before you sell an article, but your persistence will pay off in the end.' She says the ideal combination is nerve and cheek. She phoned one upmarket glossy and asked if they would commission an article on rambling. The editor said such a topic would be of no interest to their readers. However, Rhondda pointed out that rambling was less innocent than it appeared. It was rife with stories about relationships and human interplay during these protracted country walks. Rhondda's determination paid off. The editor relented and her article appeared two weeks later.

Rhondda also advises freelances to market their articles, after they have been published, to other magazines, newspapers or overseas publications. 'It means you will have to re-write parts of your articles in slightly different styles. You might as well capitalise fully on your research and spadework.'

Books and magazines

Two highly readable and expert books on freelancing are:

Freelance Writing for Newspapers by Jill Dick (A&C Black)
How to be a Freelance Journalist by Christine Hall (How To Books)

CHAPTER THREE

Putting it in Writing

Choose your subjects wisely

What is black and white, weighs less than a feather and is worth about £250? Answer: the average magazine article. With a little luck, a few breaks and considerable determination, you can make freelance writing a lucrative business. It is all a question of applying technique and know-how to a wise choice of subject matter. When you begin, this choice should be based on one, or possibly two, areas of interest. Not on five or six. Naturally, it is easier to write about something you know well such as your job, an interest or a hobby. It may also pay you to cultivate a second, saleable subject such as health, beauty and fitness; computer technology; or the environment. The advantage of concentrating on one or two subjects – instead of a miscellany – is that you avoid spreading your talents too thinly. Specialism enables you to study your subject or subjects in depth, keep up with new trends and originate ideas of your own.

How you do this varies from subject to subject. If, say, your main interest is travel, your most fruitful research source would be 'on-the-job', writing about your expeditionary experiences and the different cultures, customs, architecture and scenery you come across. You could back this up with copies of the *Blue Guides* (published by A&C Black) and *Rough Guides* (distributed by Penguin) which will provide interesting and original information about the individual countries you visit. Then, when you sit down to write the articles, get a copy of *How to Write and Sell Travel Articles* (Allison and Busby) by the travel writer Cathy Smith. It would also help you to read as many travel articles as you can, noting the different formats in the publications that carry them. You will see, for instance, that many pieces carry neat fact-boxes at the end, showing which company or airline you travelled with, your take-off and destination points and the price of the trip, as well as recommended hotels, eating places and car-hire, all invaluable pointers to the reader.

Not all subjects are as accessible as travel. You may choose to specialise in a scientific or academic subject, researching university archives and libraries and interviewing experts in your field. Or perhaps you are a keen gardener with handy seasonal tips and ideas to pass on to other enthusiasts; or a sportsperson who likes writing about your exploits as a swimmer, skater or golfer. Alternatively you may enjoy writing about personal experiences. One woman freelance writer who is married to a diplomat has a natural flair for ending up in unusual situations – even on her wedding day when, bored with the elaborate ritual of trying on wedding dresses and choosing bridesmaids' bouquets, she decided to go fishing and caught a seven-pound trout, calmly driving home and removing her galoshes two hours before the church ceremony. It made for a sparkling magazine article. Whatever you choose to specialise in, the simple message is: The more you know about your chosen subject or subjects, the more confident you will become when writing about them.

WHAT IDEAS SELL?

As a freelance journalist you will find a surprising number of sources of inspiration and ideas. Even when shopping in the High Street or supermarket, you may come across unusual events or eccentric characters to write about – the *Independent* ran a popular column called *Trolley Life* about quirky happenings in supermarkets.

One day you may be quietly reading the newspaper on the train, when an extraordinary marital dispute breaks out, so bizarre that it gives you an article idea. Funny incidents at work also make for excellent stories – and you have the added bonus of knowing the people involved which helps you to make colourful character sketches. You may come across a news story such as an accident or fire where people have been rescued or even died. By describing the incident and getting hold of the names of those involved (you will find this far easier if you have a National Union of Journalists press card), you could sell the story to a local, regional or national newspaper. Though make sure you speak to the newsdesk first, and when you send it via the copytakers, give your name and address and telephone number so you can be paid for your efforts! You could earn £50 or more for such stories.

If news is your speciality, a spell on a local newspaper plus shorthand and newspaper law will give you all the reporting back-up you need. Another good way to get the ideas flowing is to hold brainstorming sessions with friends or fellow freelances, bouncing off ideas on different subjects with each other. Whenever you think of a good idea, jot it down. Make sure you keep a notebook in the car or by your bed – a lot of good ideas come to you in the middle of the night! Also note down any witty phrases or soundbites you see or hear in the media. You never know when you might need them in an article.

How do you tell if an idea is going to work?

As soon as you get an idea, you must ask yourself:

- Can it be developed? Does it have good angles and/or easily available sources of information?

- Is there a market for it? Are there magazines, trade journals and newspapers that cover this subject or territory?

- Does the idea have a theme or angle, or is it too vague? In other words, it may appeal to you, but will it appeal to the reader?

If all the answers are 'yes', then it is a good story idea and can be pursued. If any of them are 'no', it is unlikely to work.

A guide to some hot and marketable ideas

Personal experience

The most popular topic for a magazine or newspaper article is personal experience. It could be surviving a dangerous fall while potholing, or a charming story about buying a new pet – equally fraught with anxiety, apprehension and excitement as you try to come to terms with a new member of the family. Passion and originality is what sells these stories. Be as dramatic as you please. You could write an article about 'How I gave my baby away'; if it's not yours, it could be someone else's. Or a story about living with a partner who has done a stretch at Her Majesty's Pleasure. Or, on a lighter note, perhaps the life of a primary school headmaster who was a chart-topping pop-star in the 1960s.

What makes all these stories good sellers is human interest. At its best, it can turn an ordinary story into a great one. How about comparing three couples who have been, or are about to be, involved in an arranged marriage? How do they cope with Western attitudes? What was their parents' response? How did they feel at the marriage ceremony? You could include a poignant list of whys and wherefores with all the spin-offs of race, religion, sex and relationships. Battling against adversity with alcoholism or drugs are firm favourites with editors, as are more gentle issues such as how to get on the right side of the boss, a life in the day of a double-glazing salesman, a tricky job interview, or 'How I was gazumped when trying to buy my first flat'. If you write these stories with zest and humour, the publishing world will be your oyster.

Health and beauty

Almost all of us are interested in our appearance and general well-being, and therefore like to learn about effective ways to improve these. There will always be a market for information on losing weight, putting it on, getting fit, eating more sensibly, or fending off unpleasant illnesses or infections. If you are a professional in this field – whether a beauty therapist or fitness instructor, vegetarian or naturopath – you have huge scope for article-writing. Pick up a sheaf of newspapers or magazines at the newsagent and more than half will have articles on health and beauty for men, women and children, ranging from: 'Is beauty skin deep?', 'Putting vanity before sanity', to 'Inner peace gives you an outer glow'. The huge output recently of alternative medicine ideas makes this one of the most productive sectors for freelance journalists to write about.

Money

Western capitalism has made us increasingly money-oriented. We want to know where and how to get the best prices for goods, services, houses and mortgages. We also like up-to-date tips on what to do with our money. The *Daily Mail*'s Money Mail is a rich source of advice, and welcomes well-researched articles from freelances. In fact, all the national newspapers, including the tabloids, carry money advice. There are also magazines specialising in property, mortgages, pensions, life assurance, savings and lifestyle that are always on the look-out for good freelance articles. If you work in the finance sector (or even if you don't) and are privy to news of opening markets, investment opportunities, useful and unusual tax havens, money-saving devices, get-rich-quick schemes – or even how to win the Lottery! – get writing. You could even compile a layman's guide to a life of ease and luxury!

Interviewing

Almost every article or news item is about people, so it is not surprising that there are so many celebrity profiles. However, you don't have to be famous to make a good interview subject. As a freelance you could write about the eccentricities of a flat-mate; an unforgettable person you have met; or someone with an unusual interest, hobby or achievement. Many magazines and newspapers would take such an article. If you do have a famous person who has been in the news recently living near you, he or she could make an ideal interview subject. The key is to try to get the article commissioned first; otherwise, unless your subject knows who you are working for, they may be reluctant to be interviewed (*see* Chapter 7, pp. 97–98). After you have had one article published, you can go on to do more. If you like people and are a good listener, interviewing is a lucrative source of income.

Travel

Holidays are usually for relaxing and getting away from it all. They are a good source of filthy lucre as well! The travel-conscious British love to hear about holiday locations, often the more exotic the better, so as to pander to their escapist natures! If you enjoy travel, why not put pen to paper while you are doing it? There is so much to write about – from religious rituals to unorthodox architecture and unusual events. You can also sell your photographs at the same time as your article. For some reason things tend to happen on holiday, many of which are downright comical and make great stories fit for retelling, such as someone's struggles to get through a swamp in a faraway jungle or the pitfalls of a package-holiday-from-hell.

Why not write about British places of interest? One freelance I know has sold four articles on Swindon for airline magazines! Another one, headed 'Spa Trek', described Britain's historic spa towns. You can sell photographs of your travels, which – like the articles themselves – can be recycled for different markets in Britain and overseas. If you sell 13 or more articles in a year (including recycled versions of the same article), you can join the British Guild of Travel Writers for £50 (020 8998 2223). One of the advantages is that if you get an article commissioned by a newspaper or magazine, the Guild will sometimes pay your travel expenses. When you get established, get your own entry in the *Travel Writer's Handbook*. It is where many travel editors look to find writers.

New technology

Britain is a nation of communicators. It is often easier to talk to your Australian cousin on the mobile than to have a chat with the next-door neighbour, and people are often looking to upgrade their computers or finding out new internet tricks. That is why there are so many magazines, trade journals and specialist sections in the national newspapers covering computers and information technology (IT). If you work in or have an interest in these fields, you have an excellent source of articles to tap into. The internet is a key part of the global media, with access to everything from the price of a second-hand car to the winner of the US Tennis Open. So look out for human interest angles such as 'How we met and married on a website' or 'How I found my favourite aunt in cyberspace'.

This sporting life

Even non-sporting people are often fascinated by winners and losers. If you are not a fanatical West Ham supporter, you may still feel a flicker of pride when an English (or Scottish, Welsh or Irish) team wins at something. Stories about comebacks after illness, unusual training methods, even false drug allegations make for stirring stories. How about 'A Day in the Life of a Premier League Rugby Player' – how he prepares for matches, the dressing-room banter with colleagues and the pressures of the game? Or the pressures on a national woman's rugby player?

There is a huge range of sports magazines, and newspaper sports pages, whose editors are constantly on the look-out for articles. I know a Harlequins rugby coach with a talent for writing, who was determined to supplement his income by selling stories of the sporting life by working as a freelance sports journalist. After attending a short course in journalism at a further education college, he started joining the press box at rugby matches where he met correspondents from the nationals, magazines, radio and TV – some of whom he had already come across while coaching at Harlequins. Then a *Telegraph* journalist asked him to stand in for them and report on a match. Shortly afterwards, he was asked to help out with the making of a TV rugby programme and had two stories published by *Rugby World* magazine. Soon his career progressed, thanks to canny networking. Now he is a full-time freelance journalist, writing regular articles for the rugby magazines and newspapers and contributing to TV programmes.

Animal magic

The British are not only insatiable pet lovers, they are also enduringly sentimental about them. Just look at the number of television programmes and magazine or newspaper stories about pets. In a recent survey of tabloid stories, animals came out as one of the top five subjects people like to read about over their morning coffee. If you keep a pet or pets, or are involved with animals professionally, here is a good freelancing opportunity. Snakes, chipmunks and poodles all have personalities and some very quaint and endearing habits. You could write about: 'The day my snake ended up in the neighbour's bath', or 'How Charlie the cockatoo saved our marriage'. Animals are highly photogenic – and if you manage to capture a puma lurking in the Surrey woods, you may have a news goldmine on your doorstep!

Relationships

You only have to open a glossy magazine or daily newspaper, or watch early evening television, to see how interested people are in relationships. Our interest gives ample scope to the agony aunts who try to minister to our needs in their columns. Perhaps it is because love is such a painful passion, that we laugh so much about it.

On top of the more 'ordinary' stories, you find the sensational ones about partner-swapping in the suburbs, or 'How I Fell for my Best Friend's Husband'. You can write these, without necessarily becoming a second Jerry Springer into the bargain! If you have the courage to be candid about your personal relationships, you have a fruitful little market in front of you. Reading about other people's heart-rending calamities – or successes – makes us feel more secure about ours. If you've got a story to tell, flaunt it and accumulate a nice little income into the bargain.

Humour

Do you have a gift for writing humour? It is a rare and priceless gift – publications are always on the look-out for humorous or witty stories. They can be raucous, subtle, outrageous or ironic, and they have to make people laugh. Stories can be near the bone, such as seeing the funny side of a hospital operation, or about an amusing piece of absent-mindedness, such as unwittingly reading out your notes twice during a speech. If you can remember or can make up jokes, or have had a funny experience, *Reader's Digest* pays up to

£200 for such submissions. You might find you have a gift for writing funny columns like the journalists Miles Kington or Alan Coren. So keep practising the jester's art. Alternatively, keep a file of jokes and oddities, writing them down as and when you hear or experience them. They could prove valuable.

MARKETING YOUR IDEAS

Once you have the ideas, you need to be able to *sell* them. Here are the main steps you need to take to get there.

Getting the commission

In almost all cases, you need to get your article *commissioned* before you write it. You will then know what you have to write and who for. If you send in an article 'on spec.', or unsolicited, publications may not be interested; they may find your style unsuitable, or the article too long. By getting a piece commissioned you cut out all these obstacles at the start. Remember, though, that for your first few efforts editors may wish to see examples of your writing or even the article itself before they commission it – because the magic word 'commission' means that they are going to pay you, usually even if they don't use it. The rare exception to this rule is a piece of fiction or creative writing inspired by the moment (or by the muse that has control of such things!).

Marketing it is in some ways more important than the writing of an article. However good your piece is, it is not much use if you cannot sell it. No one, apart from your friends and relatives, will be able to read it – and your hard work will end up festering in a filing cabinet instead of bringing in an equally rewarding piece of paper called a cheque. Commissioning editors of newspapers and magazines plan their schedules months in advance, and know what articles to expect and how they fit into their chosen themes for future editions. Thus, if you send in an article on spec., unless you are lucky enough to hit on a subject they are about to cover, your chances of acceptance are very slight.

Researching your article

However, even before you reach the commissioning stage, you must research your article. It may be a subject you know something about, in which case you will need to find the article's selling points to put before a newspaper or magazine editor. If it is a subject you know little about, then you will need to do enough preparatory work to produce a synopsis of what you are going to write. You will do this via libraries, databases, experts, the internet and other sources which we shall deal with later in this chapter.

It is only when the article is commissioned that you will need fully to research the article, using the angles the editor may well have suggested to you. Then, you must decide which publication or publications to approach with your article. (For a comprehensive list of possibles, consult *Benn's Media Directory*, *Willing's Press Guide* or the the *Writers' and Artists' Yearbook* at your local library). This is the market research stage. The technique I suggest you use for this I shall refer to as 'The Ten Commandments'. It involves going out and buying a selection of likely-looking newspapers and magazines, testing their suitability under the following headings:

1. Advertising
A publication's advertisers give a useful guide to the tastes and habits of their readers. The upmarket glossies tend to go for high fashion and expensive property and gadgets, while the more down-market ones use mail order to attract their readers. These will help you pitch your articles.

2. Article lengths
A recent survey by a magazine group showed that the average length of today's magazine article is about 1,200 words. Some publications prefer longer; others are happier with shorter ones. Check also to see the length of paragraph they prefer – this can vary widely. Often, they will use a very brief sentence to grab the reader's attention.

3. Brochures
Most magazines or large newspapers have a brochure and rate card which they send out to potential advertisers. Ask them to send you a copy of this. It may include useful information such as circulation, history and blurb about the publication's aims and content.

4. Frequency
How often does the magazine or newspaper come out? The cover will usually tell you whether it is a daily, weekly, monthly, bi-monthly, quarterly, annual or bi-annual publication. This will give you a guide to the kind of deadline you will be given for the article.

Monthlies like *Cosmopolitan*, *Vogue*, *Marie-Claire*, *Country Life* and *GQ* like to plan at least three months ahead.

5. Prospects

What are your chances of getting your proposed article accepted? The contents page at the beginning will usually show you how many different contributors they use. If the same group of names keeps cropping up, you know the publication relies on a pool of regulars. If the names change from week to week, or month to month, you know they use a wider network of freelances. That means there's more scope for you.

6. Readership

The company National Readership Surveys regularly supplies editors with a readership profile of all Britain's leading publications. You may not be able to get a copy of this – it is very expensive – but you could write to them for a potted version covering your own market (*see* Useful Contacts, p. 161). By studying the content of articles and whom they are aimed at you will be able to form a good idea of the age range, sex, class and occupations (i.e., lifestyle and spending power) of a publication's readers. This will help you pitch the tone and style of your article.

7. Style and treatment

Study the articles and see if they are, say, light and frothy or sharp and witty. Perhaps they have a more abstract or philosophical strain or are political, sociological and campaigning. Or are they instructional, backed up by facts and technical phrases? Most publications combine several styles, though they usually have a characteristic tone – serious or lightweight. It is also useful to know if they are lavishly illustrated with photographs or graphics – and whether they like freelances to supply these. It could earn you extra cash.

Some magazines and newspapers have a house style based on certain writing rules and favoured words or phrases. This is not a vital priority – you will generally discover this after you have been writing for the publication for a while.

8. Subjects

What subjects does the publication cover and is your article one of them? Go through several editions to find out.

9. Trends

Some magazines carry weekly or monthly themes on subjects such as health, the environment or crime prevention that your article might fit into. The current theme will be outlined in the comment or editorial, written by the editor, at the front of the publication. They may also have a Pets' Corner or a Humorous Events page that could give you a convenient slot.

10. Type

What sort of publication is it? Is it a glossy consumer magazine, or is it a more serious one? Is it a trade or professional journal aimed at a specific sector, or is it a general interest magazine? You will need this knowledge to know how to write your article.

After reading 'The Ten Commandments' above, you will now be able to compile a shortlist of publications to approach with your article.

Chatting-up editors

It is now time to sell your article, using all your powers of charm and persuasion. So, select your first choice of publication and find out the name of the relevant commissioning editor – for example, the Cookery Editor, the Gardening Editor or the Home Furnishings Editor. You can do this by checking the different sections at the front of the publication or, failing that, telephoning the switchboard and asking them.

Your next step is to decide whether to approach the editor by phone or by letter. Personally, I always favour the telephone approach as it enables you to find out immediately if they are interested. If you like putting things in writing, then outline the main points of the article and why you think it would fit into their publication in a short, concise letter. The only drawback with a letter is that it might end up in a steadily accumulating pile in the hard-pressed editor's in-tray, and you might not hear from them for weeks. A third alternative is to send a fax which, like the phone, has the advantage of directness. I would use this as the second option, to be used if you have repeatedly failed to get hold of the editor on the phone.

Before you make that crucial telephone call, write out what you consider to be the main selling points of your article. (If you can't think of any then it probably isn't a strong enough idea in the first place.) Specify why you have chosen their publication – editors always like to know that. You could say you have been taking it for some time and have enjoyed many of its articles, or that you have read a recent series they have run on, say, the environment and believe your article could be included in it. Then make a note of any bright or catchy words or phrases you can think of to help sell your article and impress the editor at the same time. (Remember, journalists like playing with words.)

Now it is time to take the plunge. Put that important piece of paper in front of you, breathe deeply and relax, then start dialling. A good time to make that call is between 10.00–10.30 am on magazines, when the editor's day is starting. They will probably be enjoying their first cup of coffee or tea and are unlikely to be in meetings or meeting deadlines. For newspapers, phone a little later, say 11.00–11.30 am. Be confident and try to smile down the phone. If they ask about previous experience and you haven't had any, say you are starting a serious freelancing career, know your subject very well, have had plenty of writing experience at school and college and are now putting this to the test by going for your first commissions. If you have had previous experience, tell them where you have been published, especially if they are important publications. Remember to take notes of what the editor says. These will prove an invaluable guide to writing the article. If you cannot get hold of the editor, keep trying, and if you still cannot make contact, send a fax outlining your proposal in about five paragraphs.

If the editor likes your idea, they will ask you to send in a short synopsis of the proposed article, mentioning a few points they may like you to highlight. Try to respond quickly by fax while your proposal is still fresh in their mind, ensuring your synopsis is short and to the point. A neatly phrased, five- or six-paragraph synopsis with several compelling reasons why your article would fit their magazine would be quite sufficient. Remember to put a contact phone, fax or e-mail number on your synopsis.

The synopsis

In summary, your synopsis should include:

- the theme of your piece;
- why it fits into the publication;
- what's new about it;
- any witty words or phrases you can think of to describe it.

Here is a synopsis written by a young freelance journalist, for the staff editor of *Guitarist* magazine. During the introductory telephone conversation, the editor had asked for polaroids to see if the guitar was photogenic.

```
Simon Bradley                          43 OAK WAY
Staff Editor                           TWICKENHAM
Guitarist Magazine                     MIDDLESEX
Future Publishing                      TW2 5JS
30 Monmouth Street
Bath BA1 2BW                           TEL: 020 8234 5678


6 February 1999

Dear Simon,

After last Friday's telephone conversation, I have pleasure in
enclosing the polaroid photographs of Tom Mates's guitar.

I bought the instrument two years ago from veteran blues player
Cliff Aungier whose CV reads like a Who's Who of modern British
guitarists. His first album, Wanderin', released in 1966, was
produced by Jimmy Page, while one of his latest, Livin' The Blues,
issued in 1988, featured such guitarists as Jerry Donahue, Micky
Moody and John McLaughlin.

The guitar is a left-handed model which I string upside down using
nine- or ten-gauge strings. Though based on a Telecaster, there are
some distinct differences. It has 22 frets instead of 21 and the
pick-up configuration is a twin coil at the neck and a single coil
just above the bridge.

I have been playing and singing as a soloist and band-player for 14
years. I also spent two years as DJ, lighting engineer and
guitarist at the famous Red Lion pub in Brentford.

I have extensive biographical details of both Tom Mates and Cliff
Aungier. If there is any other information you would like to know,
please don't hesitate to get in touch with me.

Thank you for your interest.

Yours sincerely,


Gareth Foreman
```

Note Gareth Foreman's knowledge of his subject, which the editor would obviously identify with. Note also some neat name-dropping. This is a confident letter, as Gareth had not done any freelancing at this stage.

The editor's response
As with your initial telephone call, the advantage of sending your synopsis by fax is speed – though of course, you might not be in any

hurry! A faxed synopsis will quickly catch the editor's eye, who can then respond if your article appeals. If you send your synopsis by letter, as Gareth Foreman did, the editor will often respond quickly by telephone or fax if they are taken with your proposal. You will find they usually reply this way, then confirm the conversation by letter. Don't be put off, however, if you don't get a response to your fax for several days. The editor may already have dictated a letter which is waiting in the out-tray ready to be sent. If you don't hear anything for seven days, give them a nudge by telephoning them while the article is still fresh in their mind.

When the editor comes back with a positive response, he or she will ask you to emphasise certain angles in your article and give you a specific length and deadline for the article. They may also ask you for photographs, illustrations or graphics. They will then do one of two things. They will either ask you to send in the finished article so they can read it before deciding whether to use it or not. If they do want to, they will then come back to you with a price. Alternatively, they will commission the article and tell you the fee they are prepared to pay. If they don't mention money, ask them how much they will pay for your article; then, when the amount has been agreed, *make sure the editor puts it in writing*. This gives you a binding contract confirming that the publication is using your article. You may also be able to claim expenses for long-distance travel or expensive research. Always negotiate this with the editor when you finish the article. Then when you send it in, enclose an invoice for the commission plus photographs or illustrations and expenses. One freelance I know got a commission from a magazine. However, before she finished the article, there was a change of section editor, and because the contract had not been agreed in writing, the new one refused to publish or pay for her article. If your commission is confirmed in writing, in the rare event of the publication not publishing your article, they will still have to pay for it. If you write a commissioned news story for a newspaper and they don't use it, they usually pay what is known as a *kill fee*, which is half the value of the original story.

How much will I get paid?
Fees fluctuate from publication to publication; however, the average is around £200 for 1,000 words. As the average length of an article is 1,200 words, this means you could expect to be paid around £240–£250 per article. At the top end of the scale, you could clinch

a 3,000-word commission with *Vogue* for £1,000, while a shorter piece for a small trade magazine or newsletter, with low budgets, may only pay £50. Sums for photographs, illustrations and graphics could range from around £50 to £150. For many years, the NUJ has been urging newspapers and magazines to set a standard rate of payment for articles, but editors like to fix their own fees, usually basing the amount on their budgets and the publication's fee-paying policy. These fees sometimes fluctuate and editors may pay more to regular contributors.

Now all this is assuming you have tried only one publication. If the first one is not interested in your article, try the others on your shortlist. Be careful, though, not to get commissions for the same piece from two publications. The editors won't be pleased to see it published by their rivals. The best approach is to market it afterwards, so that it can be adapted or re-worded for different publications (*see* Rhondda Cox's advice in Chapter 3, pp. 24–26). There is no harm either in approaching an editor with two or three ideas at once. Here is a guide to what you can expect to be paid on a selected range of magazines, newspapers and trade journals.

Magazines and trade journals
   Vogue: £500–£1,000 for 1,000–3,000 words
   Eva: £800 for 1,000 words (£200 per 250 words)
   Cosmopolitan: £350 per 1,000 words
   Good Housekeeping: £350 per 1,000 words
   She: £350 per 1,000 words
   Punch: £333 per 1,000 words
   Moneywise: £333 per 1,000 words
   Choice: £250 per 1,000 words
   Scientific Computing: £200 per 1,000 words
   Illustrated London News: £200
   Times Education Supplement: £150
   Times Higher Education Supplement: £150
   Optician: £150 per 1,000 words
   Practical Photography: £150 per 1,000 words
   New Law Journal: £125 per 1,000 words
   Parking Review: £100 per 1,000 words
   Plays and Players: £90 per 1,000 words

Newspapers
   Sunday Times: Money column – £250 per 1,000 words
   Guardian: £200 per 1,000 words

Daily Telegraph: Business section – £250 per 1,000 words
Glasgow Herald: £150 per 1,000 words
Scotsman: £250 per 1,000 words

Research

With the confidence of an article in the offing, it's time to brush-up on your research. If you carry this out shrewdly, it will save a lot of time, and a very good book to help you on your way is *Research for Writers* by Ann Hoffmann (A&C Black), who will guide you through this important process. You will also be influenced by the angles the editor asked you to follow-up when he or she commissioned your article. Below are some of the key research sources at your fingertips.

1. You can build up a useful armoury of your own *research sources*. One of these is the internet, which is an excellent source of reference on a considerable range of subjects, especially with the aid of a surfers' guidebook. If you have a printer with your PC or Mac, you can print out your findings too. A concise encyclopaedia (Hutchinson's and Macmillan's are good examples) is an ideal reference book for simple general knowledge queries. *Whitaker's Almanack* is full of data about central and local government and a vast range of British institutions, including the monarchy, the law, education, trade unions, science, technology, the arts, entertainment, sport, the police and the media. A world atlas is a useful geographical guide.

2. *Libraries*. Your local lending library and any nearby reference library will hold books about nearly all specialist subjects. Try to obtain a book called ASLIB, which is compiled by the Association of Information Management, and gives useful information contacts on a wide range of subjects. Photographic libraries will be able to supply illustrations for your articles. The British Library has more books, manuscripts and maps than any other library. Much of this can be obtained on microfiche. Day tickets are available. To obtain a full reader's ticket, you need evidence of identity and proof that you are a serious researcher (see Glossary, p. 161).

3. There are a number of *press cuttings libraries*, the largest of which is the Newspaper Library in North London (*see* Useful Contacts, p. 161) with copies of all national, regional and local newspapers. For a small fee, you can join The British Film Institute in London (*see* Glossary, p. 163) which has a comprehensive archive of television, video and cinema films.

4. The *press offices* of companies, public bodies and government departments will willingly send out information, especially if it involves free publicity!

5. *Universities* and *academic institutions* will prove a rich source of research for more scientific and academic subjects. They will be able to provide you with information about experts and specialists, too.

6. *Who's Who* will give you useful biographical details about well-known personalities and public figures. The ICM agency and *Stage* magazine (*see* Useful Contacts, p. 161) can provide contact details for the agents of showbiz and sports stars.

7. If you wish to trace a book that has gone out of print, you can contact one of a number of *book-search agencies*. The fastest, most efficient, and least expensive that I have used is called Twiggers, of 17 Mullins Path, Mortlake, London SW14 8EZ. Tel: 020 8878 8644. They have worldwide contacts and usually manage to find the book you want in around ten days for well under £20. You could also try Amazon (www.amazon.co.uk) which carries more than one million book titles.

There are many other valuable research sources that you will pick up, and probably keep referring to, as you go along. If in doubt, consult your local librarian for advice about where to go. Remember, it always pays to do too much research, rather than too little.

Putting it in writing

Having done your research, it is time to write the article. Here is a step-by-step guide to that process. If you have never written to deadlines before, it is a good idea to invent them when you begin writing articles. This will give you the discipline you need when it comes to the real thing.

The early Greek dramatists, Sophocles, Aeschylus and Euripides divided their tragedies into three distinct sections – a Beginning, a Middle and an Ending – and built the action of their plays around them. Today, in sophisticated hi-tech Britain, the same technique can be applied to article-writing.

- The Beginning is the first paragraph or *Intro*, the effectiveness of which will inspire the reader to read on.

- The Middle is the *Body*, which tells the reader what the writer is driving at.

- The End is the *Last Paragraph*, whose impact is geared to leave a lingering idea in the reader's mind.

The Intro

The opening sentence of an article should be eye-catching. It is the first part the reader sees. If it appeals to them, it will encourage them to read on.

Imagine you are putting a coin in a slot-machine. When it drops, the lights start flashing and the machine comes to life. The intro is the same – the *detonator* of the article.

The intro can be teasing, provocative, dramatic or controversial – and it must be pithy. You always know if you have written a good one, because the first part of the article (if not all) tends to write itself after that first explosion of energy.

There are many ways to release that first salvo, from lying down in a darkened room to jotting down a list of ideas. After you have written a few intros, you will develop your own style. Here are some pithy ones:

'Gardening is like sex – the messiest bits are often the most fun.' (Michael Leapman, *New Statesman*)

'A funny thing happened on the way to the movies – and a nasty thing inside them.' (James Cameron, *The Guardian*)

The feature of both the above introductions is *simplicity*. Yet they both tempt you to read on. If you can aim to write your intros with the same urgency of impact and economy of effort, you will do very well.

Sometimes, intros come easily; on other occasions they can follow a spell of intense effort. So how do you arrive at that eye-catching first phrase? On many occasions you can use the main point of the article. Referring back to the first paragraph of Chapter 3 (p. 14), the intro might read: 'Skin diver Jill Neville survived after spending 48 hours in shark-infested waters.' This is straightforward and unsophisticated, and makes the reader want to find out more.

As we have already mentioned, some people have been known to sit in darkened rooms until inspiration occurs. Or to go for a long walk. One good method is to write down all the most important points of the article. Then choose two or three that stand out, finally selecting the one you believe is the best. While, if you are writing the intro to a personal interview, you may find that a controversial quote by your subject makes a good opening. Finally, when you are creating your intro, do not be afraid to rewrite it until it *zings*!

The Body

If the intro is the detonator of the article, the body is the *engine*. It provides the reader with the full works of the piece, telling them what you are driving at, giving them vital information and perhaps a controversial or amusing conversation topic. Your aim is simple: to keep up the reader's interest. To do this, you should include frequent examples from real life, ideas and anecdotes.

Remember, a journalist's job is to explain, so keep your arguments compelling and your descriptions concise. Case histories of people who have been through the experiences you are describing will add depth to your narrative, while graphics and illustrations can bring a survey or event vividly to life. Journalists are entertainers as well as explainers. So throw in the occasional short sentence or spark of humour to titivate your reader.

Here are some pointers to give meat to that body:

- Give examples to sharpen your descriptions.

- Include anecdotes to give your article colour.

- Quotes from experts will give it authority.

- Case histories will illustrate and back up your arguments.

- Include photographs, illustrations and graphics to add variety.

- A blend of longer and shorter sentences will keep the reader awake!

The End

From detonator, to engine, to final firework display. Like all meaningful farewells, the ending of your article should leave a lingering impression in the reader's mind. This is the subtle distinction between *news* and *articles*. When writing a news story, a reporter is advised to get all the important facts in the first half of the story so that when it reaches the subs desk, a hard-pressed sub-editor who is stuck for space can safely cut it from the bottom upwards. With an article, however, the second half and ending are just as important as the beginning, and a funny or ironical last paragraph can give the reader an extra frisson of delight. Some connoisseurs describe it as the 'whiplash' ending.

Use the final paragraph to make a cogent summing-up of your article, or to put in an apt anecdote or throwaway line. Remember the principles of Greek tragedy and put as much combustion into your ending as you did into the intro and body of the article.

As a good example, look at this whiplash ending to an article by Victor Lewis-Smith of the *Evening Standard*, about a television programme.

'That doesn't just take the biscuit. It takes the entire Nabisco Corporation.'

Finishing and presentation

Congratulations! You have finished your article! However, the project is not quite over yet. There are two crucial, final steps to take.

1. First, *make sure your article meets its deadline*. It is almost certainly part of a carefully prepared production schedule, and a late arrival could throw this out. Why not try to deliver your article early; it will certainly impress the commissioning editor. If however you think your article is going to be delayed for any reason, telephone the editor in good time so they can make provision for it.

2. Second, you must *check that the article is the correct length*. Your PC or Mac probably has a word-count device which will do this for you. Never under-write, and if you are going to over-write, don't go beyond 50 words more than the agreed length. If the article is unavoidably long, a neat trick is to make suggested cuts (marked in the margin in biro or marker pen) for the benefit of the sub-editor.

The way you *package* your article is also very important. Here are a few key rules.

1. Use 70–80 gram, white A4 paper. This is slightly thicker than the normal, 60 gram copy paper. Using Conqueror is a waste of money.

2. Use standard typefaces (for example, Century Schoolbook or Times New Roman), rather than flowery ones, to input your article.

3. Make sure your article is double-spaced with no misspellings (remember your spell-check), and on one side of each folio.

4. Put the word count (number of words) in the top right-hand corner of the article, rounding it off to the nearest 50.

5. If you wish to keep the copyright to your article, put FBSR (First British Serial Rights) or FWSR (First World Serial Rights) under the word count. This will protect your copyright; if you don't do this, the publication has the right to re-sell your work and claim the royalties.

6. Number each page in the top left-hand corner. Put 'mf' (more follows) at the foot of each page, with 'end' on the last one.

7. Send a covering letter – including the length and price agreed – with the article, so that a busy editor knows what to expect and what has been discussed between you. (Only use the editor's Christian name at the start of the letter if you know them well; otherwise Mr, Ms or Mrs – and *not* an overly-formal Sir or Madam.)

Your covering letter acts as a written contract if there is any dispute over publication or payment (or if the editor forgot to confirm the commission in writing). Often, freelances guarantee the publication of their articles, and payment, by this procedure. It is very important to include all telephone numbers where you can be contacted, in case the sub-editors have any queries during the editing stage. Don't forget to include an invoice with your letter.

8. Enclose any photographs, illustrations and graphics *with* the article, so they don't get mislaid by a busy editor. Make sure you have agreed a price for this extra work.

9. List your main sources, together with their addresses, telephone numbers, faxes and e-mails on a separate sheet of paper. The subs can then contact them if there are any queries.

'After-sales service'

Keep up a good rapport with your editors. When you have had several articles printed by the same publication, you could suggest meeting the commissioning editor for lunch so you can discuss future projects or go on a tour of the publication. They may well suggest it, too. The better they get to know you and your work, the more commissions you are likely to get.

Market guides

The following are two of the most useful guides to potential markets.

The Contributor's Bulletin, Freelance Press Services, 5/9 Bexley Square, Salford, Manchester M3 6DB. Each issue covers around 60 markets for selling articles plus other information. The annual subscription is £16, post free, for 11 issues.

Market Newsletter, Bureau of Freelance Photographers, 497 Green Lanes, London N13 4BP. This covers handy article markets and its £25 annual subscription includes 12 issues and the handbook.

CHAPTER FOUR

Television and Radio

HOW TO GET INTO TELEVISION AND RADIO

Broadcasting is the performing art of journalism. While newspaper reporters are tapping into their terminals, relaying the day's catastrophes, controversies and curiosities into people's homes and offices via the print media, broadcasters appear at the flick of a switch. Their presence brings the news to life with a witty aside here, a concerned comment there, vivid camera shots and sounds – and the controlled cacophone of their newsrooms always in the background.

What qualities do I need?

Both broadcasters and print reporters need flair, tenacity, a facility for words and a way with people. Broadcasters also need good speaking voices and – for television presentation – attractive appearances, as well as a basic grasp of electronic gadgetry.

Only occasionally do radio and television reporters have the luxury of sub-editors or production people to check their stories; often, they have to think and talk on their feet, keeping up a continuous commentary, whether in the middle of a war zone or covering a local anti-war demonstration. The broadcasters' bulletins are usually shorter and more frequent than those of newspaper reporters and they often have to work to faster deadlines. A television reporter covering a motorway collision with several fatalities, for instance, may have to interview spokesmen and eye-witnesses and send off the *rushes* (*see* Glossary, p. 157) in less than an hour.

News desks

Reporters and correspondents work from newsrooms and are answerable to a producer, who will dispatch them on diary and non-diary assignments and liaise with district and foreign correspondents by telephone, e-mail and fax.

Diary jobs are arranged in advance via regular contacts and organisations, with more selective items such as a film preview or parliamentary debate handled by specialist correspondents. Impromptu assignments (known as *off-diary stories*) are covered immediately by phone or live, depending on the event's newsworthiness. They are fed into the newsroom by news agencies, freelance correspondents, the public, companies, organisations, and the emergency services. These assignments sometimes include 'breaking' stories when the newsdesk is alerted as an event is happening.

Which journalists do what?

The News Editor

The news editor decides which stories must be covered for each bulletin. During the day he or she will attend several news conferences with other senior executives, to check the priority of news stories. For example, bigger items will lead the bulletin, with smaller ones needing a more quirky angle – such as a milkman who goes to work in a coach-and-four instead of a milk-van; or a pet-lover who keeps a tarantula in a wooden box under the bath!

Many hard news reports also need constant updating, such as the medical condition of people badly hurt in road and air accidents, the names of victims of suspected murders or death smashes (relatives must be informed before the media can be given names), or arrests and charges made after crimes have occurred.

Much of the newsdesk's breaking news comes from television and radio agencies and the news editor must guard exclusive stories like a Trappist monk. He or she must also make sure not to miss any stories that have been picked up by rival networks.

The News Producer

The news producer decides who to send to each job. If a quiet, two-man protest about a bridge closure turns into a full-blooded demonstration with slogans and banner-waving pickets, the TV producer will immediately send out a cameraman; while his radio counterpart may decide to send a radio reporter or commission the story from an agency or local correspondent.

The producer is a link-man or link-woman. When the rushes arrive, the producer ensures they are cut to the right length, are accurate and stylish, and then orders any graphics that may be needed (for television news items). The producer also sees bulletins to air with the help of a director who, in the case of television news, looks after camera, lighting and sound responsibilities.

News Reporters and Correspondents

Unlike newspaper reporters who usually travel solo, television reporters tend to go out with a camera operator (though labour-saving camcorders, which combine sound and pictures, are being used more and more). After shooting the story or incident, they will add a commentary and then send the rushes back to the studio. With feature or magazine-style stories, the TV piece is usually planned in advance and filmed and edited at a more leisurely pace than the more pressing news story.

Radio reporters live and die by their tape-recorders. They need to be able to interview and record at the same time, adding bursts of 'wild track' – the whining of police sirens or the cries of a group of angry pickets – afterwards to give their reports more impact. They also need to know how to operate studio technology for editing and live on-air reports, and interviews when subjects come into the studio.

Production Assistants and Researchers

These are the 'backroom' boys and girls – and their job is one of the most popular starting-points for those who wish to get into radio or television. All news and current affairs programmes need considerable fact-checking. This may involve reading-up reports or newspaper cuttings, telephoning sources of information and speaking to experts. Assistants and researchers also need to find out who owns the copyright and serial rights for material used in news programmes and documentaries, which may involve getting permission to include an item or crediting the source on air. Another researching role is to find suitable interview subjects, preparing them for appearance in the studio and coaching them on the type of question they are likely to be asked.

Sub-editors

The role of the sub-editor is to rewrite, edit and present incoming reports concisely, accurately, readably, and legally. Subs work on the bigger radio and television networks and are answerable to the producer. They also write the links and trailers for news items and devise graphics, maps and captions for on-air illustrations.

Subs who work for the Teletext (ITV and Channel 4) and Ceefax

(BBC1) networks need to operate at high speeds, for the news is constantly updated in each region for the benefit of their viewer-subscribers.

Newsreaders and Presenters

Television and radio newsreaders are generally ex-reporters or correspondents. Their field experience gives them vital knowledge about news-gathering and reporting and means they can, if need be, write, re-write or adapt bulletins before going on air. They are usually picked for their clear speaking voice (radio and TV) and pleasant appearance (TV), or both, and for their calm, unflappable delivery. They must remain cool in a crisis and unfazed if there is a technical hitch or a story breaks mid-bulletin... 'News is just reaching us that a Jumbo jet with 109 on board has crashed into the Caspian Sea.'

Though presenters and newsreaders are generally authoritative in delivery, a touch of wit or spontaneity can bring a sober bulletin to life. Recent polls show that the personality and appearance of a presenter scores high ratings with viewers or listeners.

HOW DO I GET THAT FIRST JOB IN BROADCASTING?

Broadcasting news jobs need dedication and energy. If you want to get into radio, you will first need to put together a *demo-tape* (*see* p. 55). This is like a news bulletin of four or five items written, read and recorded by yourself. It demonstrates to prospective employers the effectiveness of your voice and delivery. If television is your ultimate aim, you could go into radio first and then switch, or else attend a pre-entry film and television broadcasting course. Try also to get work experience with independent television production companies – this will help when applying for jobs and may even lead to a job itself. Always keep abreast of current affairs, study the delivery of local and national broadcasters, and see what techniques are used in television documentaries.

Network shamelessly

Talk to as many people as you can in the industry. You may have a friend or relative with an important broadcasting job; pick their brains, find out what contacts they have, and see if they can put in a little nudge here or there. If you meet an influential producer at a party, college or in the workplace, ply them with charm and questions!

You may be introduced to a television cameraman who is looking for an assistant on a project he is currently working on, or meet a BBC employee who knows of a highly-recommended course you could apply for. You may pass a film crew at work in your local city, town or village. But don't just saunter by; go up to the most author-itative-looking member, who will almost certainly be carrying a check-board, and ask if you can help out by carrying equipment, making tea or working as a *runner* (*see* Glossary, p. 157). This will enable you to see the techniques of film- and doc-making (documen-tary) first-hand. Seize every opportunity that comes your way and *don't be put off by rejection*. Every bit of experience you pick up now will help towards your future career.

The *Media Guardian*, published on Mondays, carries pages of jobs. You could also try to get hold of trade journals such as *Press Gazette*, *Broadcast* or *Ariel* – which is published by the BBC – to find job opportunities in radio or television. However, whilst a glance through the *Media Guardian* may convince you that there are hundreds of jobs on offer, don't be over-optimistic. Companies are in fact statutorily obliged to advertise many of their appoint ments publicly, most of which are filled internally or by people already working as broadcasters.

Finally, try applying to the BBC and ITN annual training schemes. Although only about six places are awarded out of around 2,500 to 3,500 applicants, you never know – one of those recruits might be you. After all you don't get anywhere without trying.

Work experience
Student, community and hospital radio
Working at a radio station is the most hands-on way of learning about broadcasting. There are around 80 student radio stations attached to colleges (you may well have one at yours; contact the Student Radio Association – *see* Useful Contacts, pp. 162–163). There are also community radio stations, which are independent, non-profit-making networks that work for local projects, and hospi-tal radio stations run for the benefit of patients and staff.

Approach one of these during your year off between school and college, or during your school or college vacations. They are often looking for willing hands to help fill useful airtime. You won't be paid, but because they are not over-pressured by deadlines, your fellow broadcasters will have time to show you how to operate studio equipment and learn microphone techniques. During this period, you will be able to present, report and interview and prepare yourself for work on bigger stations later on. An army major I know is prouder of his two-hour Saturday stint on a Surrey hospital radio station than of any of his exploits in international trouble-spots.

Working on a local radio station

Your next step should be to contact as many local radio stations as you can, to ask for work experience. This will generally be for a two-week period in the summer, when reporters and presenters are on holiday, and news editors and producers can spend time to get to know you. You will be able to find out how a radio station works and experience the average radio reporter's daily regime.

The boon of work experience is that you learn on-the-job and are able to demonstrate some of your skills as a news gatherer, reporter and presenter. You also learn to work to deadlines before a sizeable audience. When the two weeks have finished, you may decide that radio is not for you and that you would be more suited to newspapers – or to another profession altogether. But at least you will have tried and satisfied yourself about working in radio.

If the stint goes well, the news editor may ask you to do another. If that is also successful, they may be impressed enough to offer you casual work or even a staff job.

A few work experience tips

You can certainly aid your career cause by observing a few rules.

- Go to the office well-briefed, having listened to earlier bulletins on your or rival stations. Make sure you have read any relevant local stories in the newspapers as well. You may have to follow these up when you get to work. It will impress your superiors if you have already grasped the basic details.

- Be cheerful and enthusiastic – your colleagues and superiors will appreciate it. If you do not know or understand something, don't be afraid to ask one of the other reporters, provided they are not in the middle of a story or bulletin. Don't muddle on blindly. That way you'll never learn.

- If you find you have nothing to do, ask for work to keep you occupied, or else offer to make the regular daily phone calls to the police, fire, ambulance and coastguards. If you are asked to do filing, make tea or carry equipment, do it readily.

- Be prepared to work longer than your allotted time if asked to do so by the producer or news editor. News stories are unpredictable and sometimes take longer than at first appeared. If a big story breaks, offer to help fix up interviews and follow-up leads.

- Good luck! The more positive your attitude, the greater your chances of success.

Making a demo-tape

Whatever you decide to do in radio (and perhaps television later) it is essential to make a demo-tape. A good way to practise is to read out items from the newspaper, asking a friend to read the cues to each piece: 'And now we move to Nicaragua, where John Fortescue has news of the recent flooding...' When you feel confident enough, record these on to a tape-recorder until you have a newsy-sounding four- or five-item bulletin. Keep tapes of work experience reports and interviews. Then, when you have a strong selection, record your *demo-tape*. You can keep updating this as and when you cover bigger and better stories. When applying for jobs, it is a good idea to tailor-make your tape to the tempo and style of the radio station you are approaching.

Working on a local newspaper

Many radio and television reporters begin their careers on local newspapers. These give you a good basic grounding in journalism, especially in news-gathering and reporting (*see* also pp. 81–84). They also help you to develop a news-sense – whether you are covering a golden wedding, a magistrates' court case, a council meeting or a murder hunt. Finally, working and training on local newspapers teaches you how to write an *intro* (first paragraph of a story) – a vital ingredient of radio and TV bulletins.

The transition from local newspapers to local radio is relatively painless. You work from a studio instead of an office, learn microphone skills instead of shorthand (though this can be useful when making background notes for films or bulletins), and practise speaking clearly instead of tapping into a computer. This is why many radio employers recruit from local or regional newspapers.

Joining a course

Work experience *makes* you do it; courses *show* you how to do it.
Employers are generally more likely to take you on if you have combined work experience with a course, and many courses include
spells of placement work. Courses are able to pass on valuable theory combined with technical information. They also help guide your
career in the right direction; for example, suggesting which companies to apply for and giving you useful contacts.

Another merit is stimulus. You will be able to meet broadcasters
and guest lecturers who can pass on tips, contacts and professional
advice, and maybe dazzle you with their televisual dexterity.
Perhaps you are lucky enough to have an inspiring tutor whose
example profoundly influences your early training, or a group of colleagues to fire your youthful enthusiasms.

Most courses are *pre-entry*, which means you learn broadcasting
skills before starting a job and can therefore try out your own film-
making and radio-recording ideas before taking the plunge. The
number of pre-entry courses is steadily growing at UK colleges and
universities, and ranges from three-year broadcasting degrees to
two-year diplomas, HNDs (Higher National Diplomas) and BTEC
courses. Always look for courses that include a sizeable chunk of
work experience. One of the best sources for courses is Skillset (*see*
Useful Contacts for details), a highly respected training organisation that produces a *Careers Book*; this covers all current courses,
where to go for training advice, and case studies of people working
in the industry. Skillset also runs its own broadcasting training programmes. The other main training body is the Broadcast
Journalism Training Council (BJTC). BJTC approves and recom-
mends postgraduate and non-graduate pre-entry courses.

NVQs

National Vocational Qualifications (NVQs) were introduced by the
Conservative Government during the recession of the 1980s. The
aim was to get people into jobs that precisely matched their skills.
They were seen as a unique form of vocational training and were
adopted by many different trades and professions, including broadcasting and print journalism (*see* pp. 7–8). They have been largely
successful and new ones are regularly starting up.

One of the unique characteristics of the NVQ (or SVQ – Scottish
Vocational Qualifications) is that trainees put together a portfolio of
their own work – instead of having to pass examinations and tests –

to qualify for the full diploma. This helps out individuals who are less examination-minded than their colleagues. NVQs usually last one year, though candidates are sometimes allowed to take up to three years, depending on the college. They are run by broadcast-trained college tutors and involve continuous assessment, evidence of your own tapes and *showreels* (your own film work) and statements from working colleagues.

Many local radio stations welcome NVQ and SVQ candidates for spells of work experience, as it enables them to use your skills free. The better employers get to know you and your abilities, the greater the chance you have of being offered a job during or after your training.

Training packages
Another career option is to get a job with a radio or television company that includes training as part of the package (BBC and ITN are the toughest but there is a host of others). You could do this by approaching the companies direct (*see* Useful Contacts for some key numbers) or answering advertisements in the three industry-led journals.

If you are still at the deciding stage...
A one or two-year Access or Foundation course in Broadcasting or Journalism at a London or provincial college or university would be an ideal way of helping you decide whether radio or television is the career for you. You can often study these part-time or in the evenings. Run by experienced broadcasters, the courses will give you essential information and guidance about the industry.

Getting in from the ranks
There *is* another way to get into broadcasting – by starting off as a secretary or personal assistant with a TV company or radio station. Many famous reporters, presenters and producers have begun their careers in the clerical department of the BBC. Let us assume, for example, you are a personal assistant to a documentary television producer who is making a doc about deep-sea fishing and needs someone with a specialist knowledge of a certain type of seaweed. It just so happens you did a botany degree at college which included a project on deep-water seaweed. So you volunteer your skills for the project. After this initial offering, the grateful producer may decide to enlist your talents again and go on to offer you a job as a

researcher. You may be working as a newsroom secretary when the producer announces that he or she needs someone with a knowledge of nuclear physics for a science story. You happen to fit the bill. Before long you may find you are bringing in the news yourself as a TV or radio reporter.

The advantage of working your way up from the inside is that you are on the spot and have easy access to jobs when they arise. Should you have an idea for an item or story, you can approach the news editor or producer directly and, as you are there every day, they will invariably use you again until you become too invaluable to be ignored. Also, look out for vacancies that are advertised internally before they go into the trade papers – seeing them first will give you a head start over external candidates.

Freelancing

Many broadcasters are now freelance. There are three reasons for this. The first is *logistical*. As companies go digital and more high-tech, machines are tending to replace people. The second is *statistical*. The BBC's emphasis on bi-media training in radio and TV means that many employees can do several different jobs at once (some BBC regional reporters work for both radio and television networks), thus reducing the need for new recruitment. The third is *economic*. The modern trend is for employers to hire reporters, producers and other broadcasting personnel on short-term contracts of between six months to two years as it is cheaper and easier to do so. Although it does not have the security of a staff job, freelancing enables an individual to work for more than one company and to develop his or her own film or radio projects. If you do decide to freelance, it is probably best for tax and marketing reasons to set yourself up as a company with your own office and facilities – or to pool your resources by combining with several other freelances (*see* Chapter 3, p. 17). Today's freelance can build a mini-studio with digital editing facilities and many of the accoutrements of the professional company, plus e-mail and internet to keep in touch with potential employers.

Rates of pay

* Producing shifts with TV news agencies pay £170 and upwards for an 11-hour day. This means a freelance producer only has to work 12 shifts a month to earn £25,000 gross, giving them scope to pay the bills and subsidise their own film-making activities.

- Terrestrial, satellite and cable television newsrooms pay about £160 for a 10-hour producing shift.

- Radio newsrooms pay between £70 to £140 a day for freelance reporting shifts.

The last word

Will Baynes, secretary of the Broadcast Journalism Training Council, offers sanguine advice:

'If you want to get into the BBC, ITN or comparable television organisations, it is essential to be computer literate, useful to have a language such as Russian, French or Spanish, and important to understand economics and to have a grasp of what scientists are talking about. If you wish to work in radio, you need to be able to talk about lifestyles as well as hard news events.'

Making it on the air

Emma Morgan is a BBC producer, but getting there was by no means straightforward. Hers is a classic tale of triumph winning over adversity.

After gaining an English and Drama degree at Hull University, followed by a post-graduate Drama diploma in Cardiff, Emma spent five years as an actor, working in the theatre with occasional commercials and walk-on television parts. However, when she realised she was not going to be the next Dame Judi Dench, Emma decided to change careers, gaining two-months' paid work experience with her local paper followed by three weeks in the features department of the *Independent* (which she managed to gain via a journalist friend). Emma then took a one-year Foundation course in Journalism at a London FE college, writing theatre reviews for the *Jewish Chronicle* and getting occasional acting parts to help pay the rent. One of her articles was published by *The Times* and soon afterwards she was offered a job as deputy editor of a newspaper about the Channel Tunnel. The newspaper folded, so Emma decided to pool her acting and journalism talents and try to get into television current affairs. She saw an advertisement in the *Guardian* for the BBC graduate training scheme. One of 3,500 applicants, she managed to get short-listed to the last 100. However they only took six trainees. Undeterred, Emma applied for a job as a *runner* – a general utility person who does all the basic manual jobs before, during and after a programme is made – with a weekly television show.

Encouraged by this experience, Emma applied for a researching job with the BBC's Kilroy programme. The interview did not go well. However, when she got home she wrote to the editor, suggesting five ideas for future programmes. Her persistence paid off – she gained a two-month contract.

Soon afterwards, Emma was promoted to assistant producer with Kilroy – again on a short-term contract. However, Emma decided she wanted to try to get a staff job. She approached an organisation called The Research Register (*see* Useful Contacts, p. 162), an agency that helps TV researchers and assistant producers find jobs. She got an interview for a BBC researcher's post. It also went badly. So she repeated her previous formula, writing letters to the programme's producer and editor with six programme ideas. It paid off – she got the job. Not long afterwards, Emma's talents were recognised and she became the producer of an afternoon current affairs programme.

Emma's advice is: 'Always talk to people whether they are friends and acquaintances, people you meet in the pub, colleagues on courses, tutors, speakers or people who work in the industry. This will build up a network of useful contacts. Then don't be afraid to approach editors, news editors and producers with your CV and ideas – the whole industry thrives on ideas and if you have good ones as well as some talent you can rise very quickly in both radio and television. Don't be too proud to work your way up from the bottom – you will pick up filming techniques as you go along, and my experience as a reporter on a local newspaper proved invaluable, as it taught me to have a news sense.'

Emma says her 'secret weapon' is her contacts book. 'While working in the theatre and on BBC's Kilroy programme, I wrote down the names, addresses and phone numbers of all the celebrities I met. This gave me a long list of people I could book for celebrity spots while working as a BBC researcher.'

CHAPTER FIVE

How to Succeed in Public Relations

A journalist going into public relations is like a poacher becoming a gamekeeper. The quarries that the journalist chased so hungrily for stories – i.e., public figures, companies, government and public bodies, charities and unions – now become his clients who pay him to protect them from predators like his former self.

In fact, it would be easy if the public relations profession could be dismissed so lightly. Public relations personnel (PRs) play as significant a role in the media and public life as journalists and broadcasters – sometimes more so. The main difference is that PRs represent clients, while journalists and broadcasters act as public messengers. There are approximately 25,000 PRs in Britain, compared with around 55,000 journalists and broadcasters. Despite their sometimes conflicting roles, they generally maintain amicable relations, the journalist helping the PR by promoting their client or clients; and the PR the journalist, by feeding them newsworthy stories.

WHAT IS PUBLIC RELATIONS?

Organisations and individuals use salesmanship, marketing and advertising to promote and sell themselves. If they do this well, orders, clients and contracts flow in. However, they usually need to cultivate the climate or market first, and this is where public relations comes in. PRs help to establish their clients' images and reputations and instill that inner glow of confidence in customers and contacts. They are the goodwill ambassadors of commerce and public life.

Much of the PR's work is done via the media. However, public relation officers use a wide range of other methods to get their messages across. These include trade fairs, exhibitions, conferences and road-shows; videos and audio-visual displays of products and services; sponsorship; stunts such as bungee-jumping or motorcycle escapades; literature such as house journals, posters, leaflets and brochures; and presentations, competitions and trade receptions. PRs not only look after the way their clients handle the customers, groups and organisations – known as *publics* – with which they are linked, they also strive to maintain a high morale among their clients' own staff so that directors, management and employees can work together in harmony.

A booming business

Public relations is a growing profession, particularly in a society where presentation is highly cherished. Most large and medium-sized companies and organisations have an in-house PR department (paid employees of the firm), or else hire a PR consultancy, an independent firm of public relations consultants, to look after their interests. Individuals such as actors, politicians and public figures tend to use publicity agents to help promote their reputations and livelihoods.

Some of the most successful PRs are as well-known as their clients. One of the most articulate is Max Clifford, a former reporter on South London's *Morden News*. He has represented OJ Simpson, Diana, Princess of Wales, Frank Sinatra, and many other personalities. Lynne Franks, the environmentalist, has successfully promoted such causes as Greenpeace, Amnesty International and the Variety Club of Great Britain; while Sir Tim Bell was hired by Baroness Thatcher to help raise the Conservative Party's profile during two general elections.

Is it the career for me?

What qualities do you need to get into PR? Put yourself to the test. If you like and are good at meeting and organising people, write well, have bright ideas and enjoy getting results, you would undoubtedly be a good candidate. You also need energy, common-sense, patience, intelligence (including analytical and strategic skills), diplomacy and the ability to put the customer first.

There are more than 9,000 PR consultancies and in-house PR departments in Britain, which are broadly divided into two sectors –

corporate and *media*. New recruits in the corporate sector start as PR assistants helping to organise events, write brochures, carry out research and assist the more senior members of the department or consultancy. In media PR, you would usually join as an assistant press, publicity or information officer, your job being to deal with the media, handle press and broadcasting inquiries, write press releases, articles and letters and help organise press conferences and receptions.

Promotion in PR tends to be rapid and posts such as Director of Corporate Affairs and Communications Director can be reached at a relatively young age. Starting salaries range from around £9,000 to £15,000 p.a., which compares with a junior reporter on a local newspaper who begins on about £9,000 p.a. Most PRs who have been in the business for five years can expect to take home more than £25,000, while the top 20 per cent are on salaries of more than £50,000. This compares with the average £20,000 salary of a senior reporter on a regional daily or evening newspaper.

You do not necessarily need a degree to go into public relations, though it can help initially. It is certainly important to take a PR diploma or PR degree at a reputable college before you apply for a job. Companies like recruits to be familiar with public relations work, and if you join one of the larger consultancies, they will send you on courses and train you on-the-job (*see* p. 73). Journalists make good PRs, particularly in the media sector, and former reporters and editors sometimes use their contacts to set up city, finance or personality consultancies.

PR and the media

PRs who handle the media are known as Press, Publicity or Press Relations Officers, Information Officers or Media Consultants. One of their key roles is to use their client's activities to gain useful media coverage. This might be anything from a change of chief executive or the development of a new product to an employee who has conquered Everest via the tricky route. It is the media PR's job to handle all daily inquiries from newspapers and networks about their clients.

To coin a popular PR phrase: it takes years to build a reputation; seconds to destroy it. Media PR is also concerned with the prevention of bad news. The methods they use are known as *crisis management*. If there is an environmental catastrophe such as a tanker capsizing and spilling its oil cargo in the North Sea, it is up to a special media response team from the tanker's owners to handle the media. They try to do this in three key ways. First, they must express the company's concern about the tragedy; second, highlight the efforts they are making to protect the public and environment from further oil pollution risks, and third, show the media they are an efficient and safety-conscious company. If the news seeps through to environmental campaigners such as Greenpeace, another team of PRs will be brought into the crisis, telling journalists of the spill's effects on marine and wildlife. A subtle dialogue will then be played out between the two companies, the effectiveness of their PR being reflected in the way the event is handled on radio, television and the newspapers.

Attracting the media
Media PRs have other methods of attracting positive publicity to their clients.

Press releases
These are information sheets giving details of an event, achievement, product or activity. Some press releases are about straightforward technical matters aimed at specialists in the national media and the trade press. Others need strong news angles to attract national journalists and broadcasters. This is where PRs who have worked in the media have an advantage – they know what makes a good story.

If possible, press releases should be written for their audiences. In other words, they should be punchy and newsy for the *Mirror*; factual and technical for the *Daily Telegraph*; expert and detailed for trade and technical journals. Sometimes press releases are *embargoed*. This is deliberate. It means the information they contain cannot be used before a specified time. This enables PRs to keep them to media deadlines and journalists and broadcasters to absorb a large amount of information.

Press conferences
Press conferences are held when an event is considered too important for a press release. The PR team invites the media to a prestigious venue such as a hotel, conference hall or the firm's own banqueting suite, so they can make their announcement live. They

then ask the organisation's chief executive, the chief press officer and one or two experts to form a panel to answer media queries, and hand out media packs (folders of facts, figures and photographs) to the assembled media.

For example, if a car manufacturer invents a revolutionary, electric-powered vehicle that has been approved by all the motoring organisations, the PR would invite the national media's motoring correspondents plus specialist magazines such as *Autocar*, *Motoring News* and *Car Choice*. They would also lend them models of the car to test-trial for one or two weeks, so they can print or broadcast reports on the cars.

Press conferences are being used more and more by public bodies and the emergency services. If, for instance, a five-year-old girl and her little brother go missing from a school playground, the school authorities and the police may hold a joint press conference. This would draw attention to the crisis and enable them to make a public appeal for witnesses, make sure journalists receive the same correctly delivered information, and – as a by-product – uphold the image of the police as an effective crime-fighting force and the role of the school as a caring institution.

Photo-calls and publicity stunts

If an event occurs that makes a good picture, the media PR will either use their own photographer or contact the media's photographers to shoot it for publication or air-time. This is known as a *photo-call* or *photo-opportunity*.

Another way to attract media coverage is a *publicity stunt*, such as a motor-cyclist trying to crash through a brick wall or a company sky-diving team trying to beat an altitude record.

The following is a story that combines all three of the above: a press release, a photo-opportunity and a stunt.

In 1998, Greenpeace staged a three-man protest about saving the Canadian rainforest. The protest was timed to coincide with the Queen performing the opening ceremony at newly renovated Canada House in London. Here is the story that appeared in the *Express* via a press release:

Queen ignores Nelson's Column protest

By JOHN INGHAM
ENVIRONMENT CORRESPONDENT

NELSON turned a blind eye to a high-level protest yesterday. So did the Queen.

Three Greenpeace demonstrators scaled Nelson's Column and unveiled a 70ft-long banner saying: "God Save Canada's Rainforest".

The protest was timed to coincide with a visit by the Queen to reopen Canada House in Trafalgar Square. But the Queen and Prince Philip studiously ignored the three men.

Canadian Prime Minister John Chretien, in Britain for the weekend's G8 summit, did notice the protestors. He made a remark to his wife Aline, who stared up at the 145ft column, then smiled and joked with officials of Canada House, which has been refurbished.

Greenpeace says Canada is allowing timber companies to destroy one of the world's most precious rainforests, habitat of endangered species. It claims only 69 of the 353 valleys in British Columbia are still intact.

Campaigner John Sauven said: "Chretien is watching his country's rainforests disappear. Many of the trees are maybe twice the height of Nelson's Column.

"It is not just some of the greatest and oldest trees on earth that are at risk but the web of life they support, such as eagles, otters, grizzly bears and the only population of the rare white spirit bear in the world."

Later the demonstrators abseiled in front of hundreds of tourists. Police said there were no plans to arrest them.

from the *Express*, 14/5/98

Though slightly rewritten by the *Express*, the message of the press release is clear. Greenpeace wrote several different versions and gained coverage in five national newspapers, in 15 other leading newspapers and magazines, and in seven radio and television networks.

Meetings and visits

A good way for a PR to build up relationships with journalists is to meet for a theatre evening or a social event such as Wimbledon, or a day at Ascot or Glyndebourne, with respective partners. Another is to host a dinner with guest speakers for selected journalists. Sometimes, PRs take a party of journalists on an office or factory tour to show them a company in action.

Letters to editors and articles
A proven publicity aid is to write a letter or article on a subject of national interest relevant to your client. For example, the benefits or drawbacks of Viagra, or the Ecu. Getting an article into a publication that is running a series about your field, asking a specialist to write in depth about a new product or idea in a trade or technical journal, or arranging for a company spokesman to appear on radio or television are all good ways to get your message across.

Company and corporate public relations
The other major sector of public relations is company and corporate PR. Like the media side, this is carried out by in-house PR departments and independent consultancies. Here are some of the ways in which PRs promote their clients:

Research strategies and campaigns
Public relations starts with *market research*. Without knowing the facts and figures behind a product, service or cause, you cannot promote it. This is where the PR assistant comes in. Their job is to check libraries, the internet, companies, trade publications, electronic databases and to carry out market research surveys to help build up information about a product or service. The company then uses this knowledge to learn about the market-place, its competitors and the types of clients (*publics*) it should be aiming at. PR campaigns are often closely allied to marketing ones. Whereas PR is used primarily to boost confidence, marketing is geared to attract sales. Sometimes the two can be linked.

Let us assume an electonics manufacturer has invented a new plastic laminating machine. Before launching the product, it runs a PR campaign to raise its profile within the business community, carrying out a nationwide survey in which it finds a network of companies on a Leeds industrial estate has been using its products for some time. The PR department then joins up with the marketing side and they send out leaflets to the 1,200 companies using their existing products. Next, they follow this up with telephone calls and find 200 firms interested in the new product. They then send machines to these companies on a two-week free trial backed by two-hour video presentations. As a result, half the companies buy the product and the manufacturer starts a national marketing drive.

Producing newsletters and bulletins

Employees enjoy reading about themselves, their colleagues and their company's activities. Well-illustrated newsletters keep staff informed and maintain the *feelgood* factor, while monthly bulletins sent via fax or e-mail will give customers, associates and interested bodies up-to-date news about a company's activities.

Videos and audio-visual displays

In the televisual 1990s, videos are an entertaining and immediate way of putting over a subject. They are particularly effective at explaining problems and issues, recording events and anniversaries, showing clients organisations at work and demonstrating products at conferences, roadshows and exhibitions. Audo-visual displays using slide and overhead projectors also provide excellent teaching aids when explaining products, services and company practices to employees.

Exhibitions

Exhibitions and trade shows give firms an opportunity to demonstrate their wares and services. A strategically-placed stand with well-produced brochures and experts and salesmen on hand to talk about products and services can attract valuable business to a company. Some exhibitions include conferences so that experts can talk in depth about the technical and scientific implications of the products and ideas on show. Exhibitions, trade shows and conferences use press officers to keep the media informed with press kits and useful background detail.

Presentations

Presentations are the life-blood of PR, and are particularly important when a company PR team is pitching for new business or giving an internal briefing. The two priorities behind a successful company presentation are to *research the customer and their requirements* and to *make sure you know the message you want to put over to them*. You can then structure the presentation round that.

As well as being smart and well-rehearsed, the best PR presenters have a little of the actor in them and, if possible, a nice line in humour and anecdote. Visual aids such as flipcharts, projectors, videos or whiteboards add eye-catching variety to presentations.

Sponsorship

Sponsorship is big business. Sporting and cultural events attract sponsorship mainly because of the lure of the television camera. So you get Cable & Wireless's logo on Test Match cricket pitches, Carling lager emblazoned round Premier League football grounds and American Express garlanded across the atrium of the Royal Albert Hall for a large-scale production of Puccini's *Tosca*. Sponsorship can also be used on a smaller scale – on menus at important dinners, trophies at award ceremonies, even books in chosen fields, just so long as the sponsor manages to catch the eye of the publics it wants to attract. Charity and environmental sponsorship help give companies a reputation for being conscientious and caring.

Specialist PR

Like most industries, PR divides itself up into different specialist sectors. Three of the most recent are the work of the *spin doctor*, *crisis management* and *political lobbying*.

'Living in Spin'

Most people have heard of spin doctors, but very few know what they do, apart from reading about them as rather shadowy figures in media gossip columns and profiles. What exactly is *spin*? The word literally means slant, i.e. putting a slant on something, while *doctor* may be interpreted as 'piecing together'. So, a spin doctor is an individual who pieces together slants on stories.

If a minority candidate unexpectedly wins a by-election, or a company's shares soar for no apparent reason, these may well have been brought about by clever spinning. A survey by John Maltese called *Spin Control* says: 'Spinning a story involves twisting it to one's advantage, using surrogates, press releases, radio actualities, and other friendly sources to deliver the line from an angle that puts the story in the best possible light.' The President Clinton–Monica Lewinsky affair was an example of successful spin, in which, in an age of 24-hour news coverage, Clinton's spin doctors were able to anticipate and mould events, interpret them, add extra information and steer journalists in chosen directions until the President finally survived.

Lobby fodder

PR lobbyists act for specialist groups – *lobbies* – such as farmers, teachers and old-age pensioners. Their avowed aim is to make sure an application or project from one of these bodies gets favourable treatment from the government or public bodies.

The lobbyist's priorities are to find out who to approach with the proposal, to brief the main parties involved, to persuade any opponents to support it, and to maintain good relations with the decision-makers. He/she generally does this by sending out literature, arranging meetings, lunches and social events with MPs, MEPs, ministers and senior civil servants and their associates; and monitoring select committees or the committee stages of bills so as to encourage or deter new legislation. In 1995, the Institute of Public Relations set up a PR Register, for members to declare their interests, as a safeguard against unfair or questionable lobbying activities.

Crisis management

More and more companies are hiring crisis management consultants to advise them how to cope with emergencies such as industrial accidents, environmental crises and product failure. One false step and the company finds its name trawled through the tabloids under harrowing headlines and propagandist pictures. The results could severely disrupt a company's trading and even put it out of business. Crisis management consultancies run company advisory sessions, organise courses and give lectures. They also stage simulated incidents using key role-players, such as the media, relatives of victims and emergency support teams, to show companies how to deal with these crucial situations. Finally, they teach executives about damage limitation skills and the need for media response teams, should an accident or emergency occur.

HOW DO I GET INTO PR?

If, 20 years ago, you mentioned *public relations* at a gathering, many people would have imagined posses of pretty young things in designer clothes whose duties hardly strayed further than looking young and attractive. This image is a long way from the truth. PR work needs skill, talent, intelligence and, above all, training.

Training Bodies

The main parent or lead body, the Institute of Public Relations, runs regular workshops on many PR subjects such as Crisis Management, Public Relations in the City, and Writing for the Press. These are open to anyone, students and professionals. The IPR also publishes a pack called *Getting into Public Relations* and holds annual Careers Days in October or November (*see* Useful Contacts).

Another important PR body is the Public Relations Consultants Association (PRCA), representing PR consultancies. This runs training courses and publishes information on job opportunities. The PRCA recently launched a recruitment service called Jobseek. Details of this are available to PRCA members on a database for £25 at the time of writing. Though it is aimed at people in the profession, it would be worth persuading a member to get a list for you. You can also read up about the PRCA's activities on its web-site (*see* Useful Contacts). If you are seeking further enlightenment, PR is the subject of many well-written books by British and American authors. A few trips to your local library would pay dividends.

Do your own research

There is no better way of getting to know the profession than to visit a PR department or consultancy for a day to see public relations in action. You may already know someone in PR who can put you in touch with a likely company; if not, telephone a shortlist that appeal to you. It will give you a valuable insight into the profession and the company may be willing to let you help out with a survey, event or press release during your visit.

Adopt the same approach for work experience; this time, however, ask if you can work at the company for two weeks. The summer vacation, when employees are on holiday, is a good time and the experience will enable you to handle day-to-day tasks and see the workings of PR over a specific period. If you show a marked aptitude or enthusiasm for the work, it may lead to another spell and even a job offer.

Network as much as you can. Your family and friends may know people who work in public relations or you may come across a PR at a party or social event. Question them closely about the job and its prospects – they may even know of one or two useful contacts you can approach.

Which sector shall I choose?

As in every other part of the communications industry, you will probably start in a junior post while you learn about the industry. If you are hard-working and enthusiastic, promotion could be rapid. Here are some of the sectors you can opt for:

- Government department, local authority or public sector organisation
- Trade union, trade association or pressure group
- Professional body such as accountancy, law and medicine
- Commercial company
- Charity or voluntary organisation
- PR consultancy catering for a variety of interests
- City or financial PR agency
- Multi-tiered corporation like BA or the Post Office
- Parliamentary lobbying
- Crisis management
- International company
- The COI (Central Office of Information), is a combination of PR firm and news agency which writes and distributes Government information

Go on courses

As in print journalism and broadcasting, new PR courses are starting up regularly. Many of them are degrees or postgraduate diplomas; however, you can also study PR part-time or at evening classes at the same time as doing a full-time job, whether it is in PR or not. One excellent option is the industry-approved CAM Certificate in Public Relations. A broad-based, one-year certificate, it covers advertising, marketing, public relations, sales promotion, direct marketing, media, research and behavioural studies, and can be taken at both further education and adult education colleges.

If you are successful, you can move on to the CAM Diploma which covers public relations in greater depth and can also be studied part-time or else by distance learning. Should you finish and pass both CAM courses, it will considerably boost your chances of getting a job. The Public Relations Education Trust, jointly run by the IPR and PRCA, also offers a distance learning qualification for would-be PRs. You can obtain details of this from the PRCA (*see* Useful Contacts, p. 165).

If you decide to study for a degree in public relations, the encouraging news is that almost all PR graduates go on to find work in the profession. To find out more about pre-entry courses, contact the IPR. They recently introduced their own Postgraduate Diploma in PR and will be able to give you a comprehensive guide to all training courses. The PRCA also has a useful list of recommended courses.

Specialist skills

Because the field is so wide-ranging, many academic specialities can be put to good use in PR. If you have a language, you can apply for jobs with international or European Union PR posts or, if you have a degree in chemistry or politics, you can approach a firm that specialises in your subject area – and most of the larger PR consultancies operate graduate entry training schemes.

Practise your PR skills

Invent a press release

Now why not have some fun by testing your skill in writing press releases.

Let's assume you are the Press Officer of Purrfect Products, a cat food manufacturer. Your department has been told by the Technical Director that the company has just produced a chocolate-flavoured food for man's second best friend. Tests on the new product have been highly successful. The company Communications Director has asked you to put out a press release for the popular tabloid newspapers about the new product. Write six pithy paragraphs to catch the news editors' eye, and don't be afraid to exercise your imagination!

'Coping in a crisis'

Now, here's an exercise to test your skills as a crisis management consultant. If you are in a group or class, choose an important industrial accident you have seen recently in the media. Then form two groups – the company PR team and the media – and, assuming the incident has just happened, decide how *you* would handle it.

To aid your researches, your company PR team could contact the real PR team involved in the incident and ask for copies of the press releases used at the time. This will help give the exercise authenticity. The media team, meanwhile, should divide up into a cross-section of national and regional newspapers, radio and television, so you can decide how each would approach the incident.

After you have done your research, each team makes a presentation to the other, both preparing a list of questions for the performers. For example, if the incident was about the withdrawal of a faulty product, the media might ask the PRs: 'Have any other of your company's products had to be taken out of service?' To make this more realistic, you could go into role-playing mode, playing the parts of media and PR response teams.

At the end of the exercise, each team can then decide how they would have approached the crisis.

A PR success story

There were no PR degree courses when **Alison Clarke** left school, so she went to university and took an arts degree. After selling Pedigree Pet Foods from the side of a lorry, she took a postgraduate diploma in PR and got a job as a PR assistant with Welbeck Public Relations. A year later, Alison's boss left and she applied for his job. She was turned down. Three months later, after interviewing more than 20 likely suitors, they decided to offer her the post. 'There was a slight prejudice against me as a woman, however after seeing the other candidates, they decided to offer it to me,' she says.

'PR had just lost its Ab Fab dolly-bird image, and though I was a woman in a male-dominated business, I worked hard and brought in new clients, so they could see I meant business. I also learned to see things from the clients' point-of-view and to find out what they wanted, rather than bombarding them with one-sided sales talk.'

Alison was headhunted by Britain's biggest PR agency, Shandwick, joining them as a sponsorship specialist. She studied her subject avidly, reading key trade and technical journals. She also scoured daily newspapers to keep up with current affairs and new technology, and to know what the press and broadcasters were saying. 'It is very important to be informed of what the media are doing, for it can affect the way you plan your campaigns,' she says. Most of her time was spent devising strategies, organising events and arranging speaking slots for such companies as ICI, Woolworths, Unilever and Nestlé. She also brought in new clients for her own company. It was not long before Alison was invited to be a partner in Shandwick, the world's second biggest public relations agency, later becoming president-elect of the Institute of Public Relations.

Tip from the top

Her advice to PR trainees is to show initiative to gain the edge on their colleagues. 'When you are starting out in the profession, make a list of companies that interest you then phone them up and ask for work or work experience. When you go on work placement, be willing to do any job you are asked to do and work late if a project needs finishing.'

Here are Alison's four keys to PR success:

- Excellent networking skills

- Knowledge – studying, reading and understanding your sector of the industry, whether media relations, financial PR, sponsorship or lobbying

- Sound judgement when making decisions

- Stamina and being prepared to work up to 18 hours a day if necessary!

CHAPTER SIX

Reporting

When a reporter brings in a scoop, a buzz of excitement goes round the office as the news editor, editor and senior executives decide how best to display the story in the newspaper's next edition.

Scoops are usually hard-won, involving much digging and probing, prying behind the scenes of an event and often doorstepping companies, individuals or organisations before they appear as exclusives with the reporter's byline and a shower of kudos from readers and colleagues.

Getting a scoop may not take as long as you think. You may go on the trail of murder hunts, major accidents, drugs raids, illicit sex rings and dramatic court stories soon after you join your first newspaper – strong stories that will help you to forge vital links with police, pub owners, businessmen and contacts of many persuasions. You may get tip-offs which don't seem to lead to much until one day, some of these names start to talk. You probe further, a few more leads are uncovered, and you realise you are on to a potentially good story. You go home, sleep restlessly, go to work as usual, giving nothing away about this smouldering ember, only returning to it after work, as you make late-night telephone calls, meet individuals in pubs and meticulously piece together your narrative. Finally, you get the break you need. Somebody talks... something unexpected happens... suddenly you have a scoop.

A nose for news

Only a few, exceptional stories become scoops. Most are simply newsworthy. So what is a nose for news? Many experienced journalists and 'bar philosophers' have passed judgement on this talent – without much success. So I will try to do better!

A nose for news is an instinct for what makes a good story. Nicholas Owen, a reporter I trained with on the *Surrey Mirror* in Redhill, had a unique way of telling whether a story was newsworthy – when it was strong enough for him to cancel an evening out with his girlfriend. It must have worked for him (though I doubt if he told his long-suffering partner); Nicholas became a *Daily Telegraph* columnist and is now *ITN* correspondent for the royals. After about six months, I started practising the same technique – with some success. However, one day I was going to the movies with a girlfriend in nearby Reigate, when suddenly the town's lights went out. No electricity, no film. I hastily drove with her to the newspaper's Redhill office to phone a black-out story to the *Evening Standard*. I picked up the phone, spoke to the copytaker, and momentarily forgetting I was sending a story, muttered 'Darling' into the receiver. The copytaker's reply was unprintable, but the paper used the piece. I revised my approach somewhat after that!

You are bound to meet the occasional sleuth who can file a sparkling story before their rivals have even started putting theirs together. You may even be one yourself, for you are either born with a nose for news, or will manage to pick up the scent after a year or so on the job.

Finding the angle

After gauging whether a story is newsworthy or not, you need to find a good *angle*. The two do not always follow naturally. The best way to find an angle is to watch other reporters cover stories and see what they do – either on the office phone or when you are shadowing them on assignments.

In your first few weeks of employment or work experience, you will almost certainly be asked to go out with senior reporters to police, fire and ambulance calls. If you are asked to do this, note the questions your colleagues ask about such items as break-ins, muggings and injury-accidents. One day you may both be asked to cover an accident. You will find that your colleague's main source of information at the scene will be the police officer-in-charge. He or she will be able to give out details of what happened and the names and addresses of the injured. Your colleague will then interview eye-witnesses.

If there has been a major incident, a press conference will be held with a police appeal for witnesses. During this, it is vital you take heed of your colleagues' lines of questioning. Note also that your fellow reporter will not be able to obtain names and addresses of any deceased from the police until relatives have been informed.

This is a rule that always applies – out of courtesy and respect for the relatives of the dead. Should the accident be the subject of criminal proceedings, and a driver or drivers be charged with an offence such as causing death by dangerous driving, the police will not give out information about the accident's suspected cause as it may prejudice the court case. This is known as *sub judice* – literally, before the law (*see* Glossary).

It is only by covering events with someone else that you will learn how to do it yourself. Always remember when you are shadowing reporters to take notes, writing out your own version of the story when you return to the office. If you have time, compare notes and see if you got the same angle as your colleague – you may even have a better one.

Let us suppose you have just visited the local fire station. You are given three items, one of which is a fire at a local school the previous Saturday night which has damaged the gym and part of a laboratory. No one has been hurt and the fire's cause is thought to have been someone carelessly dropping a lighted cigarette stub in a wastepaper basket.

You go back to the office and start writing it up as a one- or two-paragraph news item (known as a *nib* – *see* Glossary). Then, the news editor approaches. He says he has had a telephone call from a member of the public that there may have been a rescue attempt at the fire involving a pupil. He asks you to follow up this new angle. You go to the scene, and outside the school in Witchhazel Drive, Dawborough, you meet a teacher who says one of the pupils apparently hauled the headmaster to safety soon after the blaze began.

Now you have a real story. You manage to get the names of the pupil and headmaster from the teacher, and go to the local council offices where you find the boy's home address in the Voters' List (always a good source). Now you pay him a visit. He tells you that the headmaster, who was recovering from a broken leg, had tripped over while trying to get out of his study. However, the 17-year-old heard his cries for help and managed to drag him to safety. You also speak to the boy's parents who tell you how proud they are of their shy and studious son. You take this down and then leave and tele-phone the headmaster who confirms the pupil's story, adding that he cannot praise the pupil's courage and initiative highly enough in saving him from smoke inhalation and possible loss of life. The head is recommending the boy for a police bravery award.

Thanks to some digging, you have a good story. You return to the office and tell the news editor who sends a photographer to take a picture of the boy in front of the charred building. The newspaper already has a head-and-shoulders (*see* Glossary) picture of the head-master in the files. The news editor tells you he wants the story for the paper's Thursday edition. It is now Monday, so you write it up in good time to be checked by the sub-editors.

You think no more about it until Thursday, when you glance at the newspaper's front page and read: 'Shy pupil saves Head from blazing school'. It is your story, together with your *by-line* (your name – *see* Glossary).

Sources of stories

The news editor of a local newspaper is like a community messenger, receiving news of events and activities from all the main institutions and industries in that locality, many of which have their own press officers or spokespeople to pass on this information – while a few send a brief letter or make a phone call about a forthcoming function or presentation. This is how newspapers manage to cover so many events – because of their wide-ranging contacts, which include members of the public and the reporters themselves. Obviously, the national newspapers and radio and television stations deal with news on a much bigger scale; their information comes from all the major institutions such as parliament, the main law courts, the City and all the important public bodies.

In local communities, however, things are carried out on a more intimate scale. If, for instance, the British Legion is holding a Remembrance Day parade, they will ask the the local newspaper to cover it. District branches of trades unions, chambers of commerce, political parties, companies, councils and local pressure groups all want their activities published in the local newspaper – and any reporter who hasn't seen a WI (Women's Institute) report at some stage of their career hasn't lived! Many items of high, and low, drama come from the emergency services – police, fire, ambulance and coastguards. Then there is a whole host of local achievers ranging from actors, authors, musicians and showbiz personalities to explorers and sportspeople who contact the local media via their agents with news of their latest activities.

Another newsworthy group is the 'green' members of the community, known as the 'Mr or Mrs Cleans', who help preserve local parks and thoroughfares and keep them litter-free; the anti-dog and horse droppings campaigners; and eccentric political parties with names like the 'Replace Houses with Igloos' Party who stage publicity stunts and stand in general elections. Finally, an endless sequence of stories is phoned in by members of the public, such as a sudden and inexplicable plague of maggots in someone's garden, or someone's daughter who wins a university scholarship at the age of 15.

The following are three of the most important sources of news in a local community:

Councils

The councils you are most likely to cover on a local newspaper are County, Borough, District, Parish and Unitary. These are a constant source of local interest because they deal almost exclusively with council taxpayers' money! Occasionally long-winded and dull, council meetings and committees can also feature anything from high passion to low cunning. Stories about trees blocking cottage views, sleeping policemen holding up traffic and noisy builders keeping residents awake arouse very strong feelings in communities. Because they involve local politics, council meetings can get heated, so it is important to keep your reporting balanced and not be swayed by extreme left- or right-wing opinions. Get to know one or two key councillors, who will be able to give you handy tip-offs about important stories. Watch out too for the inevitable publicity-seekers!

Local MPs

Members of Parliament are at the hub of power and influence. They are also vital members of local communities. If an individual or organisation has a problem they wish to solve they usually approach one of three sources – their local councillor, their MP, or a local newspaper. The local MP, if he is an effective one, probably has the greatest clout of all three. He or she can take the issue up in parliament and, in some cases, use it to help introduce new legislation which may have an important bearing on your local area. So your MP is a prime source of community stories – read any local newspaper and you should find at least three stories about the local MPs and their activities in the area. MPs and agents are normally very prompt about contacting the local newspapers with press releases, telephoned statements or copies of speeches.

Courts

Court cases are an unending source of riveting stories (read the inside pages of the *Daily Telegraph* for some of the most sensational). These can range from murders to drugs conspiracies, armed robberies and embezzlement.

In covering court cases, a good grasp of shorthand is essential. You cannot afford to make mistakes or you might find yourself ending up in court yourself – as a defendant. Should you miss something, you cannot ask a defence lawyer to repeat himself from your cosy perch in the press gallery! So it is vital that you take shorthand classes seriously during your training. Though some top court reporters perform at speeds of up to 200 wpm, you will find a shorthand speed of 100 wpm to be quite adequate for most hearings. If somebody is going too fast, be selective; paraphrase the dialogue, only writing down key quotes verbatim. It is also imperative that you study the court reporter's bible, *Essential Law for Journalists* (Welch and Greenwood), obtainable from the NCTJ (*see* Useful Contacts). The book covers everything you need to know, from the age limit for juveniles – 17 – to why courts occasionally hold hearings in 'camera' – the press is sometimes barred from covering particularly sensitive or confidential material.

Diary or non-diary? – that is the question
Diary stories
All future events to be covered by a newspaper are kept in the office diary. These are sent in or phoned to the newspaper by local organisations and individuals. They are then handed out daily by the news editor. The diversity is huge. One morning you might be reporting the opening of a sports and social club by a local MP; the next, covering the launch of a new style of ambulance.

Off-diary stories
These are all the unplanned items of news that occur every day – from accidents to industrial disputes. Some of these are known as *breaking* stories, i.e., they are happening now. Others are referred to as *running* stories – events that keep thowing up new angles and so keep the story going and reporters on their toes! The news editor must ensure that there is a core of reporters who are not on diary stories, ready to cover these live stories.

THE STORY

The reporter's brief
When a reporter is about to go out on a story, he is usually given a

brief by the news editor or editor. This is a summary of what the newspaper wants covered, and usually consists of the basic details of the story – i.e., names and addresses of the people and places involved and any possible leads to follow-up. Often the brief also gives the reporter the *angle* that the paper wants for the story.

If the event has happened before, or is a sequel to a previous one, check the newspaper's cuttings for useful background information. Then, before you leave the office, make a list of phone numbers and addresses of useful contacts you may need to speak to while covering the assignment. Finally, check with the news or picture editor if he wants to send a photographer with you.

The check-list – five keys to reporting

Finally you reach the assignment. Here is a check-list, known as the *five Ws*, of what you need to discover for your story:

- **What** happened
- **Why** did it happen (or how, if you cannot find out why)
- **When** it happened
- **Where** it happened
- **Who** was involved

So let's apply the five Ws to the fire story above. *What happened*: there was a fire at a school. *Why (how) did it happen*: it is thought that somebody dropped a burning cigarette end. *When did it occur*: it happened on a Saturday night. *Where did it happen*: it happened in Witchhazel Drive, Dawborough. *Who was involved*: it involved the school headmaster, the firefighters and a brave pupil.

There, in a nutshell, are all the basic facts. If you remember this simple guide, it will provide the story's backbone and help you avoid missing out anything significant. Now, when you have added statements from those involved and witnesses plus some local colour, you will hopefully have a first-class piece of newspaper reporting.

Covering the event

Let us assume you have just reached the scene of a two-car accident. Both drivers have been injured, one seriously, and taken to hospital. What do you do next?

Remember: your aim is to get a hard, readable, newsy story. If there is a time limit – if, for example, the paper goes to press that day – you must produce this quickly. If the story is not time-sensitive, then you will have a little more time to forage for angles and colour.

As a rule, try to speak to the police officer-in-charge first. He or she should be able to give you most, if not all, the answers to the five Ws. There may also have been *eye-witnesses*. So you look for them as well. Then you might suddenly uncover a strong *angle*: the driver who was seriously hurt was on the way to his wedding when the crash occurred. Will the marriage be postponed or cancelled altogether? Now a *human interest* story looms and you want to get pictures of the groom without trespassing on hospital territory (he has been injured). You manage to trace a relative of his who has pictures and also knows that the bride lives locally. Then you try to get an interview and photographs of the bride, so you can run a really heart-rending story. It might even be worth selling it to one or two national papers (see *lineage*, p. 92). You note down a short description of the make, model and colour of the two cars before returning to the office. Anything else? One other thought should be lingering in your mind: what is the condition of the seriously hurt groom? You now telephone the hospital press office and discover he has died. You have a scoop: 'Bridegroom Killed on Wedding Day'.

One important tip. Whenever I covered stories as a reporter, I always marked any significant points – vital facts or key quotes from people involved – with a star in my notes. It gave me an invaluable guide to the story's highlights when I did the write-up.

Finding off-beat angles

When reporting bigger stories, you may find opposition newspapers, radio reporters and even a local TV correspondent on the scene. It is often a good idea to work together or hunt in packs, so you do not miss anything (even national reporters do it). It is also advisable to try to steal a march on the opposition, if you can, so your newspaper gets a better angle – especially if it comes out earlier than the others (though it is unlikely it could beat the frequency of radio bulletins). So look for witnesses the others may not have noticed. You will often find them on the fringes of an event and they might just have the angle you need for a strong news story. It will also give you the edge over your rivals. Even if you are the only reporter covering a story, try to find the less obvious angles, to give it more impact.

Icebreakers

It is a fallacy that the only way to get facts out of people is to play the hard-nosed reporter of fiction. As a reporter, you should be able to get on with anyone. When you talk to eye-witnesses, be pleasant and relaxed and show the common touch. Imagine you were an eye-witness and a reporter fired a lot of machine-gun-like questions at you without really waiting for an answer. You wouldn't like it and would be loath to say anything. Remember: people involved in fires, accidents and misfortunes of any kind are already worried and tense. They don't want you to add to their difficulties. So, if you need to ask a probing question, do it gently or build up to it slowly.

The same advice applies to anyone you speak to on the job – from celebrity interviewees to sources, members of the public who phone in stories to local dignitaries. The only time you have a licence to drill, is when you are following up stories where you suspect there has been a deliberate cover-up, or people are being obstructive or patently not telling the truth. If there is a lull in the dialogue, or you are not sure what to say, ask the question 'why'. It helps people to open up and often reveals a lot more than you might think. If people clam up, make your excuses and move on to the next source.

The contacts book

All the time you are covering stories, you are picking up names, addresses and phone numbers of useful contacts. These are the 'usually reliable sources' you sometimes read about. You can turn to yours for background information, news and tip-offs. They could be a regular in a pub, a loquacious sub-postmaster, a friendly police inspector or someone with a talent for being indiscreet. Fleet Street journalists used to say that many of their best stories came from the people they saw the most, i.e. taxi-drivers, hairdressers and barmen.

From the day you start out as a reporter, write down the names and numbers of useful contacts in a Contacts Book as and when you come across them, with a few notes on their jobs and interests. Then try to keep in regular contact with them for potential stories or follow-ups – one of them may come up with something special when you are short of news. The longer you work as a reporter or specialist, the bulkier your Contacts Book becomes. Newspaper job advertisements sometimes ask quite specifically for reporters with strong contacts books.

The write-up

Let's assume your first assignment was the shy pupil who saved the headmaster from the fire. You are now back at the office, perched expectantly at your computer terminal, your notebook beside you. This is the moment you must put your literary skills into effect. Your first task is to try to read back your shorthand. For the first few months, you will find that your notes are a mixture of English and shorthand. Then as you get more adept, this will become mainly shorthand. Try to write neatly in your notebook to make the write-up easier. Then, check any of the significant points in the story you marked with a star (see above, p. 83). For they might hold the key to the intro and help to give your story more impact.

The Intro

The first paragraph of a story is known as the introduction or *intro*. It needs to be catchy, dramatic and teasing enough to make the reader want to carry on with the story. Provocative, witty, controversial, pithy and condensed – any of these descriptions might apply to a good intro. Some tabloids instruct their journalists not to write more than 25 words in the first paragraph, with some stories this is not always possible, but it is a good principle.

Here are two alternative intros for the fire story. Which do you prefer?

> The headmaster of Mulberry Comprehensive School, in Witchhazel Drive, Dawborough, Peter Ridgeway, narrowly escaped serious injury when one of the school's pupils dragged him to safety during a blaze that damaged the school's gym and a first-floor class room.

Or:

> Shy Mulberry Comprehensive pupil James Hampton was hailed a hero after dragging his headmaster to safety from a school blaze.

I am sure you'll agree the second one is better. Though the first one has all the facts, it is giving you several ideas at once and does not read well. Whereas the second gives you one dramatic idea in 20 words. It is that one dramatic idea that counts – the *angle*. This is what you must aim for – to find one outstanding feature of the story and highlight it in the intro.

Then put the facts in order of importance in the succeeding paragraphs. A good guiding rule is to assume a reader is picking up the newspaper for the first time and wants to know the story in the first four paragraphs.

The Middle

Now let us follow-up the intro.

> Shy Mulberry Comprehensive pupil James Hampton was hailed a hero today after dragging his headmaster to safety from a school blaze.
>
> Teachers raised the alarm when they saw smoke seeping from the Dawborough school gym on Saturday night. Minutes later, as firefighters grappled with the fire, the 17-year-old pupil fought his way into headmaster Peter Ridgeway's study and snatched him clear of danger.
>
> A grateful Mr Ridgeway said: 'My leg was in plaster after I broke it two weeks before and I tripped over and could not get up again. Flames were leaping up round the windows and doors, and the smoke was so thick I could not see anything, so I shouted for help.
>
> 'Luckily James was in the next-door classroom, heard my shouts and with no thought for himself or the danger he was in, rushed in and managed to haul me to safety. He is a very, very brave boy and I almost certainly owe my life to him.'

There you have the whole story in four succinct paragraphs. If anyone else had been hurt or the building severely damaged, you would mention these facts in the first four paragraphs as well.

Meanwhile let us continue, and notice how the facts are put in order of impact.

> James Hampton, of Long Avenue, Dawborough, said: 'I was just about to leave the building when I heard these muffled cries coming from the headmaster's study. I saw Mr Ridgeway lying on the floor. I grabbed him and literally pulled him out of the burning building.'
>
> James's father Gerald said: 'My son is normally quiet and studious, in fact he's bordering on shy. I am very proud of him – he showed great courage in an emergency.' Added his mother Geraldine: ' James is my super-hero. He really showed that he can be cool in a crisis.'

Chief fire officer Roland Johnson said: 'The boy is a fine example to anyone who might have to face a similar situation. Though smoke was pouring through the building and bits of masonry falling around him, he just got on with the job. I am amazed how he managed to get Mr Ridgeway out so quickly – he must have been practising his fireman's lifts!'

Several items of gym equipment and part of a laboratory were destroyed in the fire, which is thought to have been started by a burning cigarette end.

Only nine people – three teachers and six pupils attending an evening seminar – were at the otherwise empty school in Witchhazel Drive. However, no one was hurt and the estimated cost of damage is thought to be around £10,000.

It will be business as usual when the summer term begins in two weeks' time. The 350-pupil school has already received several generous donations from parents who launched a fighting fund to help replace lost equipment.

Meanwhile Mr Ridgeway is recommending James for a police bravery medal and a special fire safety award for his act of heroism.

Now you have the complete story. Always try to get quotes from relevant sources, in this case the headmaster, the brave pupil, his parents and the chief fire officer. These sources give you added information and colour. Note also facts such as the extent and cost of the damage, the parents' fighting fund, the number of pupils and the vital news for parents that school will open as usual when the new term starts.

The Ending

The story also has a satisfying ending about the intrepid pupil being recommended for a bravery award. Always try to end your stories strongly. Good examples are:

- a quotation that sums up the narrative;

- an interesting or unusual fact;

- a touch of irony.

An effective finish will make the story more readable and neatly round it off at the same time. The ending is even more important in feature articles where the aim is to leave a lingering idea in the mind of the reader. Sometimes, when they are facing a deadline, subs cut stories from the bottom upwards. However, if you finish your story well they will respect this and keep the ending in, cutting other parts instead.

Does reporting improve your writing?

Reporting is a discipline. You have to marshall your facts and then write them up in newspaper and broadcasting language, a craft that can be adapted to different markets. As a rule, always try to keep your writing punchy. If you have a choice between a long and a short word, choose the short one. It is simpler, clearer and easier to read than a long, multisyllabic one! As the saying goes: 'Why use a long word, when a short one will do?'

A few critics of journalism say reporting harms your writing style. It is true there are times when you are short of space that you may have to 'bastardise' your prose a little to make a news item, headline or intro fit, but in general, reporting improves your writing. It teaches you to express yourself in different styles, stimulates your appreciation of words, writing and authors, and helps you to choose your words wisely.

What are my prospects?

When you start your reporting career, you may (if you are very lucky) get a job as a trainee on a national newspaper. However, it is more likely that you will work on a local or regional paper either as a trainee or after finishing a pre-entry course. Your official title will be 'trainee general reporter' and you will be expected to cover everything you are given.

When you finish your training period, you may decide to continue being a general reporter, in which case a varied and interesting career is in prospect. Or you may opt to become a specialist. Such a decision can often decide itself for you. You may have a politics degree and, after seeing an advertisement for a political reporter on a regional evening newspaper, apply for and get the job. Or, while working on the local paper, you did some work on the entertainments page and hear on the grapevine that the *Daily Mirror* is seeking a young showbiz reporter. Perhaps you have done one or two small items for them already, and, knowing your work, they decide to give you a chance.

Journalism is certainly a fertile land of opportunity. You may have an interest in sport and hear of a magazine that is looking for a reporter with an interest in cricket and tennis. Then you might decide to specialise quite deliberately. You may have a degree in fine arts and decide working for galleries as a press officer or as an arts correspondent on a newspaper is the career path for you – so you deliberately look for such jobs in *Press Gazette* and *The Guardian Media Guide*. One local newspaper reporter I knew decided to become a business reporter and wrote a number of stories for the London *Evening Standard* business and commerce section. Two days after his training indentures finished he got a job on the city pages and went on to have his own named city column in the *Daily Telegraph*!

You may decide that perhaps your gifts could be better used as a sub-editor in a newspaper or magazine's production department – and this is sometimes seen as a nifty route up the executive ladder. Good sub-editors become chief sub-editors and then production editors and, finally, editors. Then again, you might have a good speaking voice and decide to go into radio or television news reporting. Broadcasting employers often take people from newspapers because of their reporting experience. You may be attracted by the excitement – and danger – of being a foreign correspondent, or by the undercover activities of the investigative reporter. If you are interested in the theatre you may opt to become a drama critic.

As you can see, one of the attractions of training to be a reporter is the large number of jobs and fields you can apply for when you have finished your apprenticeship. Whatever you decide, be prepared to take a long-term view of your specialist subject or subjects. It may not all happen at once. You may have to serve a longer apprenticeship as a senior reporter than you thought, and such a role has much to recommend it. There are many local and regional reporters who are very happy to stay in the same area, with the added satisfaction of building up a rapport with the local community, away from the pressures and deadlines of the big newspapers, and perhaps writing a column about local affairs or politics. If, however, you are ambitious, remember that journalism is a competitive business and you may not always get the jobs you apply for first time. Determination is as important as luck and talent in your quest to become a successful journalist.

Joining the promotion ladder

If you are career-minded and want to get into a senior position on a newspaper, you will usually move from reporting to a job as a news desk reporter or assistant helping to receive and divide out the news to general reporters or correspondents. Your news-gathering talents could then take you to assistant news editor and ultimately news editor, responsible for the newspaper's complete news flow. This is an executive position and you will attend regular conferences with the newspaper's other executives about its content for the day or week. The next rung on the ladder on a national newspaper is assistant night editor or night editor, who oversees the overnight news production, assistant editor (news), deputy editor (who stands in for the editor during holidays and days off), and finally editor.

The progression route on a local newspaper is usually reporter, news editor, assistant editor and finally editor. There is another job-ranking system on the production side.

ANATOMY OF A LOCAL NEWSPAPER'S NEWS-ROOM

Reporting for national newspapers

Several thousand national news stories hit the news-stands and air-waves every day. These can range from the outbreak of a civil war in Sierra Leone to a protest march by the Green Party in Brighton. Where does this myriad of stories come from? The answer is a huge network of official channels, and a cross-section of unorthodox ones. In some cases, members of the public and the newspaper's own reporters and contacts pick up the latest items of news. If they do not, there is a huge second line of defence that will ensure regional and national newspapers do not miss the main news items as they occur.

The main national news agency is the Press Association, which has correspondents based all over Britain; while most of the foreign items are supplied by Reuters, Associated Press and UPI (United Press International). Independent Radio News (IRN) covers events for radio while APTN (Associated Press Television News) and Reuters provide back-up for television. All these agencies have large networks of staff reporters plus stringers (local correspondents) covering key events at home and abroad. The stories are then fed through large teams of agency sub-editors before being wired on to the relevant outlets. There are also more than 100 area-based agencies sending in news to the main outlets, the Central Office of Information (COI) which relays government news, and specialist agencies which send out photographs and news of sporting events, finance, city news, features, showbusiness and the arts.

Unlike local newspapers, the nationals have large teams of specialist correspondents covering everything from defence to the environment. Each has their own network of contacts who will supply them with press releases, copies of speeches, stories and an unceasing stream of useful tip-offs. Reporters who work in the newsroom are known as *generalists*, as they are expected to cover everything that has not been assigned to the specialists. Their reward for a good story is a byline, often with a picture if they get an exclusive. A glance through your favourite tabloid or broadsheet will often reveal stories bearing several bylines together. This is because they have been written by a team of correspondents and reporters. The most common examples of team-work items are major disasters, investigative pieces and foreign stories. When an air-crash occurs, a number of reporters will be needed to interview eye witnesses, survivors and relatives of passengers on the flight, as well as relevant authorities such as police, hospitals, airlines, relatives and foreign embassies.

Meanwhile, in another part of the country, a sleuth-like investigative reporter may be busily checking the inner workings of a dubious charity, while fellow investigators are despatched to speak to key personnel and get case histories of people who may have been conned out of cash or suffered unnecessary duress. This team of investigative reporters will then meet up and pool their facts together before writing the story under a joint byline. The best-known group of investigators is the *Sunday Times Insight* team.

In another part of the world, Bolivia, there has been an uprising, the newspaper's wires reveal. Reuters and AP are covering;

however, the paper believes the story is strong enough to send out its own a correspondent, plus a *stringer* (local correspondent) based in the Bolivian capital of La Paz, as well as a prominent freelance photographer to the scene. It also deploys several London-based members of staff to speak to Embassy officials and other Bolivian sources worldwide. All those involved will probably have their names on the news stories about the uprising.

Lineage

During your early reporting career, you may get stories or scoops good enough to sell to the nationals. This is called *lineage*. Selling news can be great fun. It will also give you the satisfaction of getting an item in a national newspaper. If the idea appeals and you do get such a story, check whether your newspaper already has a lineage syndicate specifically set up for this. It is usually run by the editor, news editor or a senior reporter acting as the local correspondent for the newspapers and/or broadcasting channels. Otherwise you can try to sell it independently. If you are not sure if your story is strong enough, ask a senior reporter to help you, perhaps offering them a cut of your fee for helping to write and sell it.

Selling stories to nationals is known as lineage because reporters used to be paid by the line. Some local newspaper editors positively encourage lineage, for it gives the paper useful national publicity and also respect as a good news source. Selling lineage can prove a lucrative supplement to your local newspaper salary, provided of course you give your paper first option on your stories. The one exception to this is when a big story breaks which the nationals are bound to pick up before your paper comes out. The more lineage you do, the better known you will become to the nationals and the greater your chances of a possible job later on.

A reporting exercise

Imagine that you are an investigative reporter on a national Sunday newspaper. You have been dispatched by the news editor to Pastures New Farm in Alfreton, Shropshire, to speak to the farmers Jim and Joan Roberts about an outbreak of BSE – or mad cow's disease – that has affected one of their herds. You have also heard that three children in Alfreton village have died of CJD, the BSE-linked disease that attacks humans; and that the local butcher, who buys beef from the farm, has suddenly gone into hiding.

Without directly linking the three incidents, write a 500-word story about the events, inventing names for the families and their children who died and remembering you cannot directly attribute blame to anyone until an inquest has been held and possible criminal proceedings started. Make up eye-witnesses and parties involved, such as a Ministry of Agriculture spokesperson, a farm worker, a neighbour and the local MP, and quote them in your story. This is a challenging test of your ingenuity. You might find *Essential Law for Journalists* useful too, as a guide!

A reporting success story

Though he wrote articles for his school magazine and a Buckinghamshire newsletter when he was 16, **Tim Luckett**'s first real flavour of journalism came when his uncle got him some vacation work on the *Mail on Sunday*. Tim, who was studying for a politics degree at Plymouth Polytechnic, spent several long weekends helping to re-write press releases, shadow reporters on stories and follow up leads at the Sunday newspaper. He then won a place on the postgraduate journalism diploma at the University of Central Lancashire, Preston, and edited the course newspaper.

After the course, Tim got a job as a junior reporter on a press agency in Leicester, going to the local law courts and covering first-class football and rugby matches, many of his sports reports appearing in the national newspapers. Despite his interest in sport, Tim made a conscious decision to concentrate on crime reporting, moving to London and doing freelance shifts on the *Evening Standard* and *Today*, and using any spare time he had to phone newsdesks with story ideas and build up contacts. He also kept up his link with the *Mail on Sunday*, working reporting shifts there every Saturday.

Tim's networking paid off. He was asked to go to the *News of the World*'s office three days a week to write the True Crime stories for the Sunday magazine. He spent the rest of his time reporting for the *Mail on Sunday* and was offered a nine-month contract running their news operation in Scotland. Then one day he received a telephone call at his Glasgow office from the *News of the World* asking him to be one of their crime reporters. He took the job only to be head-hunted six months later by the rival *Sunday Mirror*, who made him their main crime correspondent at the tender age of 28.

Tim's advice to aspiring reporters is: 'Put yourself about and offer to work free for one or two local newspapers in your school and college vacations – you can get a long way very quickly in journal-ism if you start off the right way. When you get your first job on a paper or begin freelancing, you must be single-mindedly determined and prepared to sacrifice your weekends and much of your family and social life to getting on with your career. Certainly, a very good motivation is paying off your university or college debts! News desks like reporters who sell them news, so keep phoning them with stories and ideas. This encourages them to offer you casual work and shifts, and working at different newspapers will help build up your network of contacts. It is also a very good idea to decide what you wish to specialise in, and then build up contacts in that field. Finding a niche will help you to become the master or mistress of your own journalistic destiny.'

CHAPTER SEVEN

Interviewing

THE ART OF COMMUNICATION

If you kept a record of the number of times you interviewed someone in the last six weeks, you might get a surprise. For we spend a
considerable amount of our time questioning our fellow men and
women. Of course the most common type of interview is the job
interview. You might be at the receiving end, answering questions
and trying to persuade a potential employer that you are the right
person for the job; or be interviewing someone yourself for a post.
Then of course there is that first date – those emotion-tingling questions as you ask your new acquaintance about themselves, their
interests, likes and dislikes and previous relationships before you
decide whether you want to go out with them again – and all the
time they are doing exactly the same to you!

On the other hand, there is the more practical 'interview' when
a washer goes in the bathroom tap. Unless you happen to be a bit
nifty with a spanner, you'll need a plumber to repair it. So you check
the *Yellow Pages*, pick up the phone and ask a few likely candidates
when they can do it, how long it will take and how much it is likely
to cost, before selecting someone who sounds capable and doesn't
charge an exorbitant call-out fee.

Like many worthwhile activities, interviewing is a skill. Success
as a media inquisitor differs only slightly from day-to-day interviews, your aim being to write or record a public profile of a person,
instead of a private one. If you're good at one, by applying similar
principles you'll be equally adept at the other.

Are you a people person?

If you like people, you'll find interviewing a hugely enjoyable exercise. Your subjects will be enchantingly unpredictable: some
apparently shy, but highly talkative when given a little prod; others
loquacious but surprisingly reticent underneath. It is up to the
interviewer to try to draw out the real person within, and mastery
of a few basic skills can improve the way you do this.

As an 'inquisitor' you are in a powerful position. You can ask your subject practically any question you like, within reason – though it may not guarantee you get the answers you want for your newspaper or radio profile. Sometimes people are combative and the interview becomes a game of cut-and-thrust. Others like to have the upper hand and try to dominate with their own prepared agenda. In this case, it is up to you to steer the interview back to the topics you wish to discuss. There are also interviewees who are a positive delight to talk to, warm, humorous, witty and forthcoming. All you have to do is sit back, smile and ask a few questions and the interview seemingly takes care of itself.

Interviews – sometimes referred to as *talks* – are always enriched by the people involved, whether interviewee or interviewer. The American actor Humphrey Bogart said: 'The best technique is to make tiny pricks in the subject's ego and let him expel air slowly!'. This may work for some people. Generally however, it is best to be gently absorbed by your subject and ready to adapt, chameleon-like, to their views and whims.

Exercise

Here is a little exercise to start you off on your interviewing career: Write down the names of the three people, alive or dead, that you would like to interview most, giving reasons for your choices.

Who makes a good interview subject?

Most people like talking about themselves and appearing in the media – provided it is for the right reasons. It flatters their egos and enables them to show their friends, relatives and workmates their fifteen minutes of fame.

Here are some excellent ideas for interview subjects:

Achievers

Someone who has done something outstanding, such as row the Atlantic single-handed or win Gold at the Olympics. Or, an explorer who discovers a rare species of animal; a local politician who has been promoted to the Cabinet, the author of a best-selling book, or an amateur actress who wins a West End part.

Famous people

Anyone who is in the public eye – from scientists to actors and musicians. They make news when they have achieved something noteworthy or said or done something controversial. Also, former celebrities who used to be in the limelight and have disappeared from public view make for interesting 'where are they now?' subjects.

People with unusual interests
People with unusual or interesting hobbies or pastimes, particularly if they are in the public eye, whether locally or nationally.

Individualists
Leaders of campaigns, pressure and minority groups, people in the news for their actions and views.

Eccentrics
Extraordinary or unusual people such as fire-eaters, collectors of unusual specimens or people who behave in a comical manner.

Arranging interviews
Arranging the interview needs as much diplomacy as the talk itself. In some cases, you will be able to contact the subject themselves, pointing out why you wish to interview them, the publication you work for, and then arranging potential times and dates. In others, you will need to contact their secretary or agent, giving them two alternative dates and confirming the agreed date and time in writing. For example, the chief executive of your local borough council, known for his dynamic efficiency and rough, sometimes ruthless, treatment of staff, turns out to be a rare moth collecter. He would be a suitable case for treatment! However he is a busy man, so you would need to speak to his secretary, rather than the man in person, to arrange the interview. She will then be able to ask him if he is willing and check his current availability.

Not everyone wants to speak to the press. Big personalities, in particular, are sometimes notoriously publicity-shy. So don't pursue them, unless you happen to know a friend of theirs who might give you an introduction or you are prepared to spend weeks phoning and sending faxes and e-mails to their agent in an effort to tie them down. Perhaps these exploits could make for a good interview angle in itself! Handling celebrities is a specialist task. If you don't know who is acting for them, approach *Stage* magazine's customer service department who will have the names of most well-known actors' agents. The ICM agency also acts for a large number of actors and sports celebrities. (See Useful Contacts for both sources). If they are not already handling them, they may tell you who is if you are polite and tactful. Usually the more prestigious the publication you work for, the more likely the celebrity is to talk to you. Agents or PR people sometimes sit in on their charges' interviews. This means you may have to use a little extra charm and persuasion to get a good 'talk'.

Usually, you will find that most potential interviewees are only too happy to talk to the media, particularly if it leads to some career-enhancing publicity.

Be prepared

The scouts' motto 'Be Prepared' is one of the keys to interviewing success. You must do your homework before the interview, both on your interviewee and on their subject, plus any friends, relatives or colleagues who may have some interesting insights to reveal about them. If, say, you are talking to a flamboyant scientist who has been in the news recently for his controversial views about the effects of the ozone layer on Londoners, you will need to have information about both his scientific and his personal background.

The better briefed you are, the more your subject will want to open up to you. They'll be impressed you know so much about their subject and even more flattered you know so much about them! You do not have to be an expert; just gather enough working knowledge about their subject from libraries, databases and other experts to be able to understand it and use some of the main technical words and phrases. Then, check out your interviewee in the cuttings and any recent write-ups by rival publications, ask your colleagues about them, and consult *Who's Who*, libraries and biographical literature produced by their company or PR.

Question time

It is essential you take a list of questions to the interview with you. This will keep you on track and prevent any long, embarrassing pauses during the dialogue. As you get more experienced, you may only need to write down half-a-dozen questions. Having questions ready-prepared makes you relaxed, confident and brave enough to go off on another tack if need be.

The feel-good factor

Here are some useful tips for the interview.

• Make sure you are on-time, preferably early.

- Be smartly dressed – neither over- nor under-dressed.

- Be relaxed. Interviewees much prefer to talk to someone who is at ease than nervously chewing their biro or fidgeting.

- Break the ice. Don't plunge into the interview straightaway, but make some small talk so your interviewee can lighten up.

The interview

Here are some important pointers for interviewing:

Time

You may have agreed a time limit for the talk. Keep to it.

Listening

When you are interviewing someone, make them feel important. Ask a question, then give them time to answer fully without interruption. Only nudge them back on track if they happen to stray off the subject. Two of the best interviewers are Michael Parkinson and Sir David Frost. Their strengths are that they are interested in people and are good listeners. They ask a question and listen, letting the interviewee have their say. Nearly all Frost's Sunday morning interviews are quoted in the next day's papers.

Here is an *Evening Standard* extract about Frost's interviewing technique:

Frost's compelling knack

I heard the City correspondent of a national broadsheet interviewed on Radio 4 the other day on the subject of Nick Leeson. Why did Sir David Frost get the interview, he moaned, rather than Paxman, Humphrys or one of the others with "teeth"?

The City journalist failed to realise the consummate skill with which Frost sets about his task and gets his man. "The best operator in the business," Walter Cronkite once said to me, of the man who has a legacy of more classic interviews (Nixon, the Shah, Savundra) than anyone else on British television.

Why is Frost's laid-back, at times infuriatingly lazy style so effective?

Why, week after week, does he set the headline agenda for Monday's broadsheets with his Sunday morning interviews with the hot news figure of the day?

First, he spots his target and markets himself to them with great facility. Then the victims choose to go on with Frost because they think they are in for an easy ride. No rottweiler nastiness or telepundit pomposity from David. Finally, he charms them, and then – wait for it – he gives them all the rope they need to hang themselves.

He is not the type of interviewer whom a restless audience hears talk more than the interviewee. How much did we see of him in the Leeson interview? Very little.

His often languid questions are set to elicit answers, not to express the questioner's opinions. That's why Frost's interviews are compelling.

Don't be showy

The other great interviewing asset of Parkinson and Frost is that they are genuinely interested in what their subject has to say. Their questions are aimed to elicit answers, not to show how clever the interviewer is. Some journalists and broadcasters seem to be more interested in their own questions than in their subject's answers. By all means be a little teasing or suggestive when you are interviewing, so as to obtain some interesting, provocative answers and keep the conversation going – but don't turn it into an ego-trip.

Questioning

Keep your questions short and simple. Your interviewee will only get muddled if you make them long or complicated.

Fact-checking

If you are unsure about something your interviewee said, don't be afraid to ask them to repeat themselves. Or, if you missed something or want to check a fact after the interview, telephone them. They will be pleased to help and won't think any the less of you.

Shorthand

'How do I ask questions and take notes at the same time?' is a question posed by many a new interviewer. The answer is: 'Quite easily.' You will find after the first half-dozen talks it becomes second nature. 'Do I use shorthand or dictaphone?' is another common question. The answer is both. Taking notes concentrates the mind and helps you to think. If your shorthand speed is not yet developed, you can always ask your subject to repeat themselves or to go a little slower when you are taking down a good quote. Using a dictaphone will also help you cover any points you may have missed. If you only use a dictaphone, your concentration tends to wander, and you may miss a good angle or comment, and transcribing the interview back takes three times as long with a tape. If you are working for radio or television, you will record the interview, editing and cutting the content afterwards. Some investigative reporters carry a hidden microphone in a pocket or case.

Some tricks of the trade

An interviewer is like an amateur psychologist trying to prise as many revealing nuggets as possible from their subject. Getting your subject to be relaxed enough to make indiscreet, candid, or controversial remarks is one of the trophies of good interviewing. They may also give you a good news angle by telling you information that has never been published before. This is the cream of good interviewing and comes from treating your subject gently and tactfully, asking them all sorts of polite and friendly questions about themselves and their activities, thus encouraging them to open up to you.

Here are two tried and tested tricks of the trade.

- If you want to get something revealing out of your subject, ask a question, then put down your notebook. Ask another question that you are not particularly interested in getting an answer to, then write down the reply they gave to the *previous* controversial question!

- Feed words into their mouth. If there is something you want them to say, say it youself, such as: 'Do you think extending the licensing hours has turned Britain into a nation of alcoholics?' To which James Burton, MP for Hinklewood, says 'Yes.' So you can say quite plausibly in your interview: Hinklewood MP James Burton says extending the licensing hours has 'turned Britain into a nation of alcoholics'. If he says 'No', of course, you can forget it.

Getting quotes from people
As a reporter you spend much of your life interviewing people either face-to-face or on the phone.

A good telephone manner
If you want the bare facts of an event, such as who did what to whom and why, the telephone is the perfect source because the person on the other end has to give direct answers without embellishment. This is why the phone is often used for routine calls to check recent events from the police, fire and ambulance services.

Face-to-face
The advantage of interviewing people face-to-face when you are reporting, is that you can give colour to your report and add descriptive details. All interview profiles should be conducted face-to-face, unless you are short of time or have a deadline to meet.

The write-up

If an interview doesn't go well, you have a chance to redeem the situation with the final write-up or broadcast. Any blips that occurred can be smoothed out during the writing or recording process and you can still produce a finely polished product.

Interviewing exercises
First exercise

Now try your hand at interviewing. If you are in a class of students or with a group of friends, divide the group into threes – one to act as *interviewer*, the second as *interviewee*, and the third as the *observer*. The interviewee then chooses a subject he/she would like to be interviewed about.

Now begin the interview, preferably sitting round desks or tables. Spend 20 minutes on the talk between interviewer and interviewee, with the observer writing notes and awarding marks out of 10 on his or her colleagues under the following headings:

- Body Language (Are they sitting upright? Are they facing one another? Are they looking each other in the eye? Are they using their hands expressively?)

- Confidence (Do they have a calm, measured delivery?)

- Enthusiasm (Do they express themselves in a lively manner?)

- Expressiveness (Are they articulate? Do they use words well?)

- Clarity (Can you understand what they are getting at?)

Change roles after twenty minutes.

At the end of the exercise, compare notes and see how you can improve on your own interviewing techniques.

Second exercise

You are sent by your news or features editor to interview Josie Roberts, an 18-year-old girl who works in a local car seat making factory. She has just won a major role in a West End musical. Josie, who is a member of the town's amateur dramatic society, was spotted by a national talent scout when he came to watch a recent production.

Write a 600-word profile of Josie Roberts and her success story.

THE ART OF COMMUNICATION   103

Then, name any other sources you might speak to about her new-found success – and suggest a suitable photograph. (*See also* Appendix 1 – Suggestions.)

CHAPTER EIGHT

Features, Reviews, Columns and Leaders

When the author Matthew Arnold wrote that 'Journalism is literature in a hurry', he was describing English newspapers in the nineteenth century. However, Arnold's remark is even more apt today. For the daily news we absorb is written at great speed and is often less literary and flamboyant than its nineteenth-century predecessors. The gripping headlines and arresting reports we wake up to about the previous day's murders, robberies, volcanic eruptions, earthquakes, foreign coups, strikes, and political scandals are often written and assembled in less than two hours as they travel from reporter to newsdesk to sub-editor and then to the final, finished page. We are the end-users of a non-stop, 24-hour word factory producing thousands of tons of newsprint each day.

FEATURE WRITING

Choosing your best feature

One section of the newspaper that doesn't have a perpetual race against time is the *features department*. Rather than bombarding us with hard news from around the globe, it produces entertaining and thought-provoking articles on issues behind the news, the arts, hobbies, fashion, people and showbiz. These are aimed to keep us entertained, amused and informed when we are not watching television or tuning in to our favourite radio programme. The department is run by a *features editor*. On larger newspapers, editors are responsible for different sections such as the arts, fashion, books and showbusiness. Underneath these senior journalists is a team of sub-editors who edit and lay out stories on the feature pages.

Where does the copy come from?

Instead of receiving most of their stories from agencies, press officers and members of the public, most arts and feature articles are devised by the journalists and editors themselves or commissioned from freelances. News reporters sometimes refer to feature writers as 'wimps'. This is simply not so. News reporters bring in the goods in a macho environment where facts are king and sensation often queen; whereas feature writers, many of whom are former reporters, tend to have a more detached, less rushed, attitude to their work and their features are less time-sensitive than news.

What qualities does a feature writer need?

Many feature writers start out as reporters, and, finding they have a gift for self-expression, begin embellishing their reports with a more descriptive turn-of-phrase. There is no doubt that many of the best use the reporters' fact-grasping skills and ability to find out who did what to whom and why, after which they have more time to develop their subjects and write with flair. Reporters also move into features departments because they wish to specialise or else have grown tired of the daily treadmill of deadlines and hard news. Others leave newspapers altogether for magazines where the pace is more gentle than daily or weekly newspapers and good writing is positively encouraged.

Newspaper and magazine features departments possess an air of fun and camaraderie. Ideas and comments are constantly batted to and fro in an intimate cocoon of gossip, irreverence and general banter over the absurdity of it all. One moment the television critic is digesting the daily dilemmas of the agony aunt, the next a general feature writer is swapping yarns with the gossip columnist.

So just what are the roles of the journalists in the features department?

General feature writers

Reporters who cover everything are known as *generalist* reporters (see previous chapter). In the same way, feature writers who cover everything are called general feature writers. They are sent out by the features editor to write general interest articles and *colour pieces* (descriptive articles about a news event). A typical scenario might be the aftermath of a train crash, with a large number of fatalities, at a level crossing in a rural village. The reporter covers the news event;

the feature writer paints a picture of the tragic scene.

The story might go something like this:

> Hoxton is a sleepy Surrey village where nothing usually happens. The postman delivers eggs for the farmer; the dry-cleaning lady has a tea party on early closing day and the High Street is so tiny that no self-respecting traffic warden would dare show his face.
>
> The village slept peacefully until last Monday when its rural calm was shattered by the ear-splitting sound of two trains colliding.

And so it goes on, describing the rural scene and the cathartic effects of tragedy.

Typical topics

Here is a breakdown of the main topics a feature writer could be expected to write about:

- interviews with local and national figures;
- descriptive pieces about new and unusual companies and organisations, ideas, inventions and products;
- anniversaries of anything from famous bands to World War events;
- people's achievements, such as climbing a mountain with a wooden leg or circumnavigating the globe in a giant balloon;
- investigative stories into corrupt organisations and individuals;
- vox pops (surveys with the man-in-the-street) about topical issues.

One of the pleasures of being a feature writer is that it gives you the scope to express your views and see your name in print. Feature writers often become well known in a relatively short time, with invitations to appear on television talk shows or panels of experts, plus all the other perks of being a somebody.

REVIEWING

If you enjoy music or the arts, tell your news editor or feature editor. Practically all reporters are asked to cover amateur theatre productions during their training, which is a good way to learn about the theatre, especially if you wish to go on to be a full-time critic. If you like music, there'll probably be local gigs you could volunteer for and you might get to talk with the band's singer; similarly, with art exhibitions and private viewings. It is only by visiting and writing about them that you can acquire a reasonable level of expertise, and artists often have original views, which makes them excellent interview subjects.

How do I become a reviewer?

Covering local events is the best way to start your career as a reviewer. You may also have professional theatres, music venues or art galleries in your area, helping to give you a jump-start to your reviewing future. There is nothing like a free night at the theatre with a partner (complimentary tickets are sent to newspapers by theatre PROs, as it give them useful publicity). An important regional concert hall in your town may give you the chance to write about classical or jazz music. Certainly, if you're a film buff, your local cinema will give you ample chance to practise your skills. Some of the best reviewers began their careers on a local paper before moving to the glamour of the national newspapers and magazines.

A good way to learn about your subject – and to find out who's hot and who's not in Hollywood, the theatreworld and the music business – is to write previews of events or shows on your local or regional paper's entertainments pages. Begin by rewriting information sent in by sponsors, advertisers or organisers. Then move on to interviews with big performers as and when they visit your town, especially when there is a local angle (for example, if they live or were born in your area).

Be a 'culture vulture'

Journalists who work on broadsheet newspaper feature pages are often 'culture vultures'. That is one of the reasons why there are so many sections with names like *The Information, The Review, Arts and Books*, and *Culture*. Every national has a separate televison, radio and video section, listing future events with interviews, previews and in-depth features, and there is a growing core of radio and television magazines. As you can see, it is a fruitful field for a young journalist to exploit. Your energy, enthusiasm and interest could lay the foundations of a bright career. Opportunism knocks!

How to write a Theatre Review

'The best judge of a feast is the guest, not the cook.' (Aristotle)

Good drama criticism is like good wine. It appeals to the senses. Just as a fine vintage of burgundy caresses the palate, a sprinkling of wit, erudition and insight tickles our 'culture buds'.

There is no mystique about the theatre. It is after all a copy, and sometimes a fantastical one, of real life. The way to approach it is like that of a reporter covering an event (*see* Chapter 6, pp. 82–83). Only with a drama review, you have greater scope to express your opinions than in a hard news report.

Put yourself in the mind of the reader

When you begin reviewing, you should try to put yourself in the mind of your newspaper's typical reader. Imagine what their likes and dislikes are – and never make the mistake of being precious or a bit of a purist. People like you to be human and fallible in your opinions – unafraid to be a little biased, even controversial, some-times, but not to be too politically correct. You don't want to end up with the kind of report you might expect to find in the minutes of a parish council meeting!

A little knowledge...

When reviewing the theatre – or indeed art, music, films, television, opera, ballet or books – it helps to have some knowledge of your sub-ject. Studying English for A-level or for a degree will give you a head-start as a drama critic. Reference books such as *The Penguin Dictionary of the Theatre* by John Russell Taylor or *The Readers Encyclopaedia of World Drama*, published by MacGraw-Hill and obtainable from libraries in four volumes, are invaluable guides with vital information about stagecraft, voice production and the use of props. However, there is no substitute for reading a play before you go to see it. This isn't always easy. It may be sprinkled with stage directions or lack the narrative flow of a novel. It will however help you grasp the basics and plot of the play so you can concentrate on the action when you go to the performance. Finally, practise your art. The more plays you see, the more adept you will become at writing about them.

Simply the best

Michael Billington of the *Guardian* is probably the drama critic's drama critic. He knows more about the theatre than most of his ilk and writes about it in an informed and spirited way. Here he is writing about a production of Sophocles' *Electra* with Zoe Wanamaker in the title role: 'With her curving, half-moon mouth and retroussé nose, she does not resemble the familiar idea of a tragic heroine. But she compels our attention... offering a mixture of obsessive grief, sexual disgust and overpowering filial love.' Billington's *Critics' View of British Theatre* (1971–1991), published by Nick Hern, gives invaluable insight into recent theatre. Another useful guidebook is *1956 and All That: The Making of Modern British Drama* by Dan Rabellato (Routledge).

One key piece of advice. When you are reviewing amateur productions, bear in mind that the cast and crew are doing this voluntarily. They will almost certainly have day jobs, spending much of their spare time rehearsing, making props and assembling the set. Try to treat their performances sympathetically and give praise where it is due. It is simply not possible to judge their efforts in the same light as a West End production.

The art of celluloid

Film reviewing is slightly different from drama criticism. It does not need the same depth of knowledge, but it does need a grasp of the modern film scene. It relies far more on camerawork and plot than the more subtle nuances of live performance and stagecraft.

To be a successful film reviewer, you need to love films and to be a bit of a celluloid buff. You need to know recent film history, the development of different genres such as the growth of the Hollywood industry, the French cinema of directors such as Jean Genet and to be able to define a Spaghetti Western.

If you wish to make a career of it, then a study of film techniques and the lives and repertoire of the leading directors and actors of the last 20 years would be required reading. Then, spend your free time watching films and videos, noting interesting or unusual sequences for future reference. A good grasp of current affairs, plus erudite opinions about culture, politics and society will help bring your film reviews to life. The doyen of modern film critics is Alexander Walker of London's *Evening Standard* who has an exhaustive knowledge of the industry. His reviews would be a good source of reference for your own criticism.

As with drama criticism, try to build a picture of your typical reader, their likes and dislikes and leaven your criticisms with wit.

Here is *Mirror* critic Donald Zec's slightly unkind but witty view of Elizabeth Taylor in the film of *Anthony and Cleopatra*: 'Fifty-seven varieties of cleavage scarcely adds up to a performance.' A neat technique is to establish your own star system, ranging from 'Outstanding' to 'Poor', awarding a golden globe to a great film and a wooden clothes-peg to a no-goer. And a final piece of advice to movie reviewers: never give away the ending!

Armchair reviewing

Most of us are armchair reviewers, indulgently praising or dismissing a weekly repertoire of television soaps, series and documentaries from the comfort of our sofas. Inside knowledge is essential and, should you become a professional armchair reviewer, you will be besieged by blurbs, programme information and news releases about recent events in the industry. Nearly the whole population of the UK watches television at one time or another, so if you try your hand at reviewing make your observations as diverting and original as possible. Also, be topical. As with film reviewing, observe how programmes fit into the contemporary scene. Three national newspaper critics who are masters (or mistresses) of the art are the award-wining Nancy Banks-Smith, Jaci Stephen and Thomas Sutcliffe. They are good for different reasons: Thomas Sutcliffe for his intelligence and observation, so that a reader comes away from his reviews thought-provoked; Jaci Stephen for her wit and candour; while Nancy Banks-Smith is always endearingly lively. Here she is at her funniest: "Ballykissangel (BBC1) was back with its very own sweating statue – like the moving statue of Ballinspiddle. Which reminds me of the photographer from the *Irish Times* who was sent to take a picture of the Moving Blessed Virgin of Ballinspiddle. 'Did it come out right?' said the picture editor. 'Ah no,' said he. 'She moved.' "

Being a good listener

Radio reviewing is another comfy-chair art. Because it is unseen and one-dimensional, critics of the radio need a vivid imagination plus plenty of topical knowledge (much of this can be obtained in press releases and information packs from the programme-makers). One of the most readable and perceptive radio critics is the award-winning Gillian Reynolds of the *Daily Telegraph*. Read her work and see how she makes her reviews walk off the page and live.

The joys of a good plot

The role of the book reviewer is to tell your readers what they can expect when they buy a new book. Books, especially hardbacks, are not cheap – costing anything from £4.99 to £40 – and your average newspaper or magazine reader needs to be told if a book is worth its price.

When you review a book, make sure you read the blurb on the back to give you a guide. Then open it up and read it. If you are pressed for time, try to take in meaty chunks until you have the gist of what the author is getting at, their style, and whether what they say is readable. You could also 'skim read' – bounce off certain points on each page – to take in a book. Whatever you choose to do, highlight points of interest in a notebook as you go along.

The author and former *Sunday Express* books editor Graham Lord says: 'My policy is that I should cover the most important and interesting books for a middlebrow readership, write a feature that can be understood and enjoyed even by the literary layman, say what the book is about, give some extracts from it, and say whether I liked it and why. Anything else is an ego-trip by the reviewer.'

This is a simple, direct analysis. As with all reviewing, don't try to be cleverer than you really are. The reader will find you out. Try to stick to three rules: What is the book about? Is it a good read? Is it worth the money? Finally, don't give the whole plot away and spoil it for the potential purchaser.

Music criticism

Music critics are music enthusiasts. To cover classical or jazz concerts, you need to know your composers and have a reasonable ear for music. If pop or light music is your bag, apart from being a trendy rapper, you need knowledge of bands and the current scene. As with all reviewing, music criticism should be audience-driven. The people who read pop columns are pop enthusiasts, while reviews of Wagner's *Die Fledermaus* will be sampled by opera buffs. In both cases your job is to tell the reader how good the product is and whether they are getting their money's worth – not necessarily an easy task, given the high prices of opera tickets!

After the film *Shine*, its subject, the pianist David Helfgott, partially overcame many years of nervous illness to revive his career with a world tour. Unlike most of the critics who tried to compare Helfgott's brilliant, if erratic, performances at the Royal Festival Hall with those of famous contemporary artists, the *Evening*

Standard's critic, Rick Jones, said with disarming simplicity: 'The ovation was immediate and who is to say undeserved? Helfgott making music is a man at his therapy and good luck to him. Comparisons with other pianists are irrelevant.'

Reviewing art

Reviewing an art exhibition is like writing a descriptive essay. You may not know the difference between Degas and Da Vinci, but you need to be able to describe what you see. If you are sent to an art exhibition with only a meagre knowledge of art or the subject on display, remember the five Ws. Who is putting on the exhibition? Why is it being put on? Where is it being staged? When does it begin and end? And what is being shown (*see* also p. 82). If you see a particularly striking abstract, put your own interpretation on it. Everyone else will. Art is highly subjective. Your role is to inform the reader and give them a taster. Don't try to fool them by betraying knowledge and insight you haven't got – anyone who knows about art will find you out.

Local newspapers are always interested in the activities of local people, so when you go to a local exhibition or private viewing, try to get an interview with the artist or some of the artists exhibiting. This will give your story added piquancy.

Rules of reviewing

Here, then, is a potted guide to reviewing. Answer the following questions:

* Where is the event being held?
* What is its title?
* Who is the author, composer, director, designer or artist?
* Who are the main players?
* What is the theme or plot?

Then tell the reader:

* If you liked or disliked the event or book
* Why you liked or disliked it
* What its merits and defects are

- Is it worth seeing, hearing or reading?

- And finally: Is it good value for money?

WRITING COLUMNS

Column-writing is one of journalism's most sought after jobs. It is also one of the hardest. Columnists come in three categories. First, the *celebrity* whose name attracts an audience, though the words may not always match the drawing power; second, the *seasoned journalist* who knows his craft and what appeals to his audience; and third, the *specialist* who writes a column about a theme such as gardening, health or politics.

Putting on the style

The hardest part of column-writing is consistency. You may have to produce a highly readable 1,000-word, five-times-a-week newspaper column and find that on some days the prose flows, on others it ebbs – though an impending deadline is a wonderful motivator! When you start writing a column, it takes a while to develop your own style and format. After that, the job becomes easier.

Study other columnists and see how they handle their topics. You will note that they often write about several subjects, ending with a short and witty item. Two of the most readable – and consistent – on national newspapers are playwright and author Keith Waterhouse, whose columns have appeared in the *Mirror* and *Daily Mail* for many years; and the jazz musician and writer Miles Kington who has written columns in the *Independent* and *The Times* for a long span. *The Times*'s Bernard Levin used to be the doyen of the breed and he is still famed for an 86-word sentence he once wrote in a column.

Here is an intro from Miles Kington in the *Independent*:

> This column is guaranteed to be an election-free zone. If any customer can find a trace of contamination by election matter, he will get his money back. Thank you.

This is a teasing opening which immediately draws the reader in. It is as if you are having a one-to-one conversation together. And that is the real secret of column-writing – talking to your readers, understanding their needs and knowing what makes them laugh or cry.

One columnist who had the ability to write for almost everyone was the post-war *Mirror* columnist 'Cassandra', or Sir William Connor (he was knighted for his journalism). His columns are still as fresh as they were when he wrote them in the 1940s and 1950s. Here he is talking about gardening:

> I hate digging. I can endure mowing, a bit of hedge-clipping, a modicum of planting and a short spell of weeding. I am at my best in a greenhouse – hidden from the outside world by the foliage of tomatoes and drinking a bottle of beer while reclining in a deck-chair. But I hate digging.

Everyone, gardener or non-gardener alike, can identify with this.

One good column-writing technique, I find, is to have a typical reader in mind. Imagine you are writing a letter to a humorous and eccentric aunt. You enjoy the exercise because you know what interests her or makes her laugh. You also know you will receive an equally comic and diverting letter back. It is the same with column-writing, only you are then writing for several thousand aunts.

A sure sign you are getting through to your readers is the size of the postbag you receive each week, letters that can make excellent column subjects in themselves.

If you do decide to try your hand at column-writing, you must choose your subject or subjects. Do you want to write about yourself and your experiences? Or maybe you have a pet hobby or interest that would make a good theme or a job that has some amusing or diverting moments. Here are two exercises to whet your columnist's appetite:

Exercise 1
Write 500 words about something interesting, funny or unusual that has happened to you in the past few weeks, in the style of your favourite newspaper or magazine.

Exercise 2
Create your own named column about a subject that appeals to you, giving it a title to start it off. Here are a couple of examples: Mrs Cohen's Cookbook; Dennis' Deeds of Derring-Do. Write it in the style of a newspaper or magazine and keep it to around 500 words.

Some useful books
Here too is a collection of entertaining columnists' books.

Alan Coren Omnibus (Robson Books, 1996)

I Couldn't Possibly Comment, Matthew Parris (Robson Books, 1997)

I Should Say So, Bernard Levin (Jonathan Cape, 1995)

Love It, or Shove It, Julie Burchill (Century Publishing, 1985)

Cassandra at his Finest and Funniest, Sir William Connor (Paul Hamlyn, 1967) – obtainable from book search firm, Twiggers (*see* Chapter 3, p. 43)

Diaries and agony columns
Though jobs on national newspaper diaries occasionally fall to well-connected Oxbridge graduates whom the diary editor thinks knows names in high places, they are in fact excellent training grounds for journalists who like writing, people and gossip, in that order – especially after they have done a stint of reporting.

Newspaper or magazine diaries have launched many a journalistic career and they certainly teach a young journalist the value of a good Contacts Book. The ex-directory telephone number of a famous film-star or director is like gold-dust in a newspaper office. The diaries on the popular tabloids and even the more serious broadsheets know that, despite their reserved exteriors, the British have an insatiable appetite for gossip. Diaries also feature highly in magazines, especially the social diaries of *The Tatler*, *Vogue*, *Country Life* and *Harpers and Queen*. So, if diary-writing appeals to you, there is a wide market to aim for.

The number of agony aunts (and uncles) that try to reassure us from the columns of their popular newspapers or magazines continues to grow in counsellor-conscious Britain. They are usually professional journalists with a sympathetic ear, who are performing a literary social service by encouraging people to talk publicly about their problems which they then leaven with constructive and readable advice. If you are a good listener – a bit of an amateur psychologist even – this could be a fruitful field for you. Why not practise with your friends and colleagues before trying your skills in print. The results could be revealing!

LEADER WRITING

Leader writers are like modern-day essayists. Their job is to give a general view of what the newspaper is thinking on a given political or social issue or event. Leaders need to be general without being personal, and pungent without being flowery. They also need an air of authority, for the paper is attempting to direct its readers as to how they should think about a current topic. Newspapers often feature two or three subjects in the same leader column, though sometimes the subject is so strong that it takes up the whole column.

Naturally, the styles of leaders vary from newspaper to newspaper – from the forthright tabloid to the more analytical broadsheet. Newspapers often like their graduate or non-graduate trainees to help write leaders, so you may well be given a number of leader-writing opportunities when you join your first newspaper.

Here are two leaders written on the same day in *The Times* and *Sun*.

THE SUN SAYS

People power

WHEN 120,000 Sun readers demand that the Pound must not be scrapped, all sensible politicians should listen.

This is the Voice of The People, shouting loud and clear.

What the Government must be made to realise, however much it might bruise their egos, is this: Those 120,000 people are the tip of a huge iceberg.

And one day, Captain Blair and the Good Ship Euro are going to collide with it.

Then he will see that it is possible to sink the unsinkable.

Your remarkable protest vote proves that Britain will not be conned, bounced, duped, prodded or pushed into something it does not want or need – the euro.

People understand that joining the single currency would signal the end of this country as an independent nation that had control over its laws and taxes.

They know that if we join the euro, there's no going back.

They're not daft, Prime Minister.

And they won't let anyone treat them as if they are.

It's their country, their currency – and their right to choose their future.

No politician is mightier than the people.

White faces

WHAT happened to Stephen Lawrence's parents was appalling.

While they grieved for their murdered son, the police treated it almost as if it didn't matter.

Their incompetence and callous indifference meant the killers have never been brought to justice.

That is inexcusable. But it does not justify a witch-hunt of the entire police force.

So we welcome many of the initiatives set out in the Macpherson report.

And Home Secretary Jack Straw was impressive in the Commons yesterday.

He was **RIGHT** to condemn racism.

He was **RIGHT** to extend the hand of sympathy to Stephen Lawrence's parents – sitting in the public gallery.

Yet the fact was if you looked around you, there were few black faces.

None in the Press gallery.

Hardly any on either side of the Commons.

And few in the public gallery. One or two in the seats reserved for Lords.

Yes, Straw was right to demand an end to racism.

But, by God, this country has a long way to go before we reach that aim.

THE LAWRENCE LEGACY

How to harness wisely the momentum of reform

Even after all the long preliminaries, the leaks, the reconstructions, the theatre, the campaigns, it is impossible to read the report of the Stephen Lawrence inquiry without succumbing to grief and anger. The waste of a promising young life, the evil that motivated murderers, and the incompetence of those charged with investigating this crime are, severally, enraging. Taken together, they form a bleak indictment of the nation's failure effectively to tackle racism. Those who have had to live with that failure for six years, and without the admirable son they loved, fully deserve the nation's sympathy. The dignity of Neville and Doreen Lawrence as they have tried to bring their son's killers to justice has been an inspiration. The desire to make amends for their loss is powerful and rooted in decency. But emotion, however noble, must not be allowed to sweep every other consideration from its path. The Stephen Lawrence Inquiry Report makes 70 recommendations, many of them overdue, but not all wise.

Anger has, understandably, found a focus in the Metropolitan Police's grotesquely incompetent handling of the murder investigation. The police's failure to deal effectively with the criminals responsible is shocking. But, now as earlier in the week, justice is still not served by the demand that the Metropolitan Police Commissioner, Sir Paul Condon, should serve as a scapegoat for unassuaged grief. He has squarely accepted the criticism levelled at his force by Sir William Macpherson of Cluny and his team. Sir Paul was understandably reluctant to accept the blanket condemnation of his force implied by the initial accusation of "institutional racism". But he yesterday showed a mature appreciation of the flaws in the police service which were highlighted by the inquiry.

The police's failings are not best understood when viewed solely thorough the prism of race. Society as a whole has been ill-served by the police service's failure to reform its recruitment, training and operational practices. It is certainly true that recruitment from ethnic minorities has been woeful, but it is also worth noting that recruitment of talented graduates from every background has been remarkably poor. The police have failed not only to reflect a changing society, they have also failed to implement the managerial reforms which other public services have embraced. It should never be forgotten that this inquiry was made necessary by the police's failure to apprehend murderous criminals. Reform must concentrate on enhancing the operational effectiveness of the police rather than seeking to conciliate every interest group with a grievance.

The police still enjoy a level of public esteem and trust which forces in other nations envy, as Sir Norman Fowler pointed out in the Commons yesterday. But past complacency has allowed that trust and esteem to erode. Reform guided by enlightened liberal principles could limit the prospect of future failures.

Respect for liberal principles should also inform the Government's reaction to some of the inquiry's more ambitious recommendations. The proposal that individuals acquitted of one crime could be retried for the same offence, if new evidence is uncovered after the acquittal, is profoundly illiberal. It could allow the persecution of individuals by prosecuting authorities who felt the howl of public outrage at their back. Also disturbing is the suggestion that a racist incident be defined as "any incident which is perceived to be racist by the victim or any other person". It should be for courts to exercise their settled judgment in assessing whether or not an incident is racist, not victims, however anguished. Justice depends on respecting the rights of victims, but those rights do not include elevating the victim to the judge's bench.

Most disturbing of all, perhaps, is the suggestion that the use of "racist language" should be considered a criminal offence "where such conduct can be proved to have taken place otherwise than in a public place". Criminalising the private expression of opinion, however offensive, would constitute a remarkable curtailment of an historic liberty. As Sir Norman Fowler wisely observed yesterday, those who legislate in anger often live to regret it. The anger which Stephen Lawrence's death still provokes is amply justified; the reform of the police is transparently justified; but erosion of traditional freedoms is not justified at all.

Note the differences. The *Sun* is emotive and personal, imploring its readers to back its Euro-cause. *The Times*, however, is more calm and dispassionate, appealing to reason with longer, succinctly stated sentences.

Now try your hand at writing a leader on a current issue – first in the style of a broadsheet, and then as if you were writing on a tabloid.

CHAPTER NINE

Sub-editing

If you tell a friend or relative you are a sub-editor, they will probably assume you are the second-in-command of your newspaper or magazine. The very title makes it sound as if you are important enough to be the assistant- or deputy-editor. A pleasing assumption, but a wrong one. A sub-editor in fact has the same status as a reporter. The difference is that a sub works on the production side, editing, cutting, re-writing and laying out stories before they go to press, rather than on the reporting or news-gathering side.

Sub-editing (or *subbing*, as it is known) depends on the dual talents of accuracy and speed. Subs are the 'hatchet' men or women of the newspaper, magazine and broadcasting worlds. They must cut all incoming stories and pictures into shape and then finely hone them ready for final printing or airing. Every sub-editor must be both observant and meticulous, able to spot a spelling error, an incorrect fact or a far-fetched statement at the drop of a megabyte.

Subs are not sub-human

Sub-editors spend most of the day in front of a computer screen and, unlike reporters, do not go out and cover stories or do much writing apart from headlines, picture captions and the blurb that appears below headlines (these are known as *standfirsts*). Though they are not responsible for finding and reporting the news, they need to be good writers, able to rewrite any sloppy prose or badly put-together stories. They need to have a thorough grasp of current affairs and knowledge of a wide number of subjects so as to cope with the huge variety of stories they edit. Above all, subs must be versed in media law – especially copyright, libel, contempt and privilege – for they are sometimes faced with contentious and controversial stories and – apart from the editor and the publication's lawyer who 'legals' tricky stories – they are the last line of legal defence on a newspaper or magazine.

Why become a Sub?

Subs serve two main roles. The first is known as *copy-subbing* – cutting, re-writing and editing stories. The second is *production*. This is designing and laying out the newspaper or magazine for publication. The production role usually falls to the experienced sub, who has already served his tenure as a copy-sub and has acquired a good eye for typefaces and the laying out of pages.

So why become a sub-editor? Newspaper journalism recruits usually start off as reporters on local newspapers, while those who join trade journals or magazines often take up subbing relatively quickly after serving their apprenticeships as editorial assistants. It is only when they have been in journalism for several years that most newspaper reporters decide to become sub-editors. There may be several reasons for this: perhaps the reporter is not a natural writer, is more interested in production and design than in reporting, or wishes to find a quick way up the executive ladder. Newspaper executives generally reach the top via the production side, though the current ratio of national newspaper editors is 50% from production and 50% from reporting and news editing. If you become a sub, it helps to have been a reporter, for it is easier to handle news copy if you know how to cover and write up events.

Job opportunities for Subs

The role of the sub has grown in importance over the past ten years. Today's newspapers and magazines are designer-led. This is partly due to technical sophistication. It is also a studied attempt to appear glossier, trendier and more user-friendly than your competitors and to fend off the rival attractions of radio and television. So, the emphasis is on appearance. Supplements continue to multiply and, aided by continuously updated software, most newspapers bedeck their pages lavishly with colour pictures, tints, cut-outs, silhouettes and clever graphics.

The good news in today's enterprise culture is that if you can sub, there is little reason for you to be out of work. Publishing companies of all sizes and persuasions are always seeking competent part-timers or freelances to cope with their increasing workloads. Magazines, trade journals, and local and national newspapers with their growing range of supplements, rely on competent cost-saving casuals to do much of their subbing and production work. On some newspapers, subs work as page editors, doing the copy-subbing as well as laying it out afterwards on screen. Another innovation is for reporters to sub and fit their own copy on the page, though this can prove error-prone as it cuts out the middle-man.

Most newspapers and magazines like prospective freelances to work initially for two paid days on the publication. Then, if they like what they see, they will ask you to come in more regularly, and when a vacancy occurs you will often be their first choice. Sub-editing is at its peak. More than half the production journalists on national newspapers are freelances, and some hold down very responsible positions. Many newspaper and magazine subs go on to form their own publishing companies, producing newsletters and magazines for large firms and organisatons.

Promotion prospects

If you are an ambitious sub, the progression route on newspapers and magazines (and in some cases, broadcasting) is to start off as a news or features sub-editor, maybe moving into sport or business subbing. You then become a *revise* sub, checking and correcting the general subs' copy. Next in line is the *copy-taster*, who casts a final sharp eye over stories before they go to press.

We now move into the realms of the executive. A fully-fledged sub can be promoted to deputy chief sub on a news, features, business or sports desk, standing in for the chief sub when he is on leave. He or she is usually responsible for the desk's weekly or monthly rota, and is likely to inherit the chief sub-editor's role. The chief sub is in charge of the desk and goes to regular news and content conferences with the publication's other executives. Chief subs go on to become production editors – at the helm of the publication's production process, which on newspapers is usually followed by night editor, assistant editor (news, features, business or sport), and finally the power-crazed heights of editor.

A magazine journalist would tend to go from production editor to deputy editor or editor. On the reporting side, reporters can work their way up by moving on to the newsdesk, which receives and divides out the news, as a news desk reporter – moving on to assistant news editor, news editor, editor, assistant editor (news), deputy editor and finally editor.

What skills do I need and how do I acquire them?

The first skill a sub needs to acquire is how to cut copy. Your first sight of a story will be when you receive it on your computer screen from your chief sub-editor or copy-taster. Before doing anything else, you should read through the story for sense and general clarity. It may be a verbose and complicated report of a council debate that doesn't make much sense on first reading. So read it through again, and don't be afraid to do this, even highlighting on a piece of paper one or two points you think are important. This will help you edit the end-product into readable shape.

Remember also to check the source of the story. Is it from one of your own reporters, an agency or perhaps another contributor? This will tell you who to contact in case of a query. Never be afraid to check uncertain facts or spellings with reporters. If you can also maintain a friendly rapport with them, so much the better. It will help make both of your jobs easier, and there will be times when handling scoops or *splashes* (big stories) that you need to rely on each other's expertise, especially if you are facing a deadline when a story must be checked quickly.

Your next task is to cut the story to length. You do this by keeping the main points, cutting out superfluous phrases or colour, rewriting clumsy or long-winded sentences, and making sure the story keeps to its theme. Competent editing skills are gained through practice. You will certainly find it easier if you have already worked as a reporter and learnt the mechanics of story-writing.

A subbing exercise

Here is an exercise to start you off on your subbing career! The following story has a number of misspellings and punctuation errors. See how many you can spot.

The famous Hampton Court Palace maize has got itself into a bit of a tangle.

The popular tourist atraction, which has managed to lure several well known public figures into its dark, inner receses, has been dismissed as a 'blot on the riverscape.'

A report by a panel of palice experts says: 'The maize is too wild, its hedges overgrown and its trees too haphazard for such a historic lanmark'.

However the maize, originally planted for King Wiliam of Orange in 1690, will be spared the proverbial chainsore.

For the experts are recomending that it be re-planted, with a new shail and brick pathway running through its centre and 50 you trees to 'fill the gaping holes that have made it such an eyesaw.'

You should have found 15 errors (*see* answers in Appendix 2, p. 168).

Good spelling and punctuation should be second nature to the competent sub. There is nothing worse than opening the pages of your favourite newspaper to find errors or misspellings. There is no excuse – all modern computers have spell-checks.

Clarity and brevity

The next stage towards subbing competence is expression. You must make sure you use phrases in a concise and readable way. This may seem an obvious statement, but it is not always easy to do this consistently. As in the cutting stage, root out tired cliches, hackneyed sentences and clumsy phraseology. Never be afraid to re-write a sentence – even if it's from a reputable reporter – to make it clearer to the reader and to yourself. This is another reason why you should read through stories twice. It enables you to grasp what it is driving at. Then you can concentrate on the language and expression.

The only time when you should think twice about cutting and re-writing is a personal column or piece of description by a well-known author. Then if, despite their reputation, you think they are writing gobbledegook, ask your chief sub or revise sub for a ruling. In general, brevity is the guiding art of journalism. The phrase 'Jesus wept' is a masterpiece of compact writing. It is simple, sad, short, and highly effective!

Here are three rules for the competent sub.

1. Don't be afraid to re-write.

2. Cut out all unnecessary words and careworn cliches.

3. Make every word tell.

Another exercise

Sub the following story, selecting the most important point for the intro, then cutting and re-writing the rest into four paragraphs.

Heathrow Airport has published proposals to tackle sharp practices by some cab drivers and improve the airport's taxi service.

They include plans to scrap the controversial local journey system, which gives cabbies a place at the head of the queue if

they return within 30 minutes. This encourages some drivers –
who prefer the more lucrative fares to central London – to inflict
a 'white knuckle ride' on their passengers, or even switch them to
another cab outside the airport, so they can get back in time.

Another proposal would see the Taxi Feeder Park abolished,
and a new state-of-the-art computer system introduced to cut the
time cabbies spend waiting for a fare.

There are fears the proposals will face anger from many cabbies who vigorously guard their independence.

Gerald Courtney, secretary of the London Black Taxi Drivers
Association, said: 'We welcome any proposals that protect passengers against the cowboy cabbies. Many of these drivers are
unlicensed. They simply get in their cars, drive to the airport and
spend half-a-day earning a quick buck at the expense of the
licensed cab-drivers. One person had to be taken to hospital with
a suspected heart attack after one such ride.'

A Heathrow Airport spokesman said: ' It is our genuine desire
to work in partnership with the taxi trade to create a core of
drivers who provide excellent customer service to our passengers,
and to get rid of the white knuckle taxi rides that some operators
inflict on their passengers in their efforts to get back to the airport
and to the head of the queue. The new system is fairer and will
enable all airport cab-drivers to earn a good living from Heathrow.'

John Daines, secretary of Independent Taxi Cabs, said: 'This
new computer system will make life even more difficult for us.
There is nothing wrong with the 30-minute local journey system
– it gives local passengers value for money. It looks as if the airport authorities are trying to push us out of a job.'

The new proposals are to be introduced on September 1.

Your story should read something like this:

The 'white knuckle rides' suffered by Heathrow mini-cab passengers will soon be a thing of the past.

For London's main airport is to abolish the controversial
scheme that puts cab-drivers who carry fares in under 30 minutes at the head of the queue.

Many fares have ended their rides trembling – one was taken
to hospital with a suspect heart attack – as the cabbies race to get
back to the airport in time to pick up wealthy customers.

Now the airport is to introduce a computer to replace the

queueing system that locals call an 'outrageous practice'.

However John Daines, secretary of the airport's independent taxi cabs group, says: 'There is nothing wrong with the 30-minute local journey system – it gives local passengers value for money.'

Note that not a word is wasted. Instead of 11 paragraphs, the story has been condensed into five, far more readable ones.

Writing the headline

After the cutting, re-writing and editing stage, we come to perhaps the most creative part of sub-editing: writing the headline. This may come to you very quickly; on other occasions it may be a struggle against the clock.

Here are a few tips:

1. Headings, particularly in news stories, are often held in the intro of a story. If you take the above story, the most dramatic phrase is the 'white knuckle rides'. Thus the heading, which you would take from the intro, could be:

'White knuckle' cabbies banned by Heathrow

2. The best way to learn headline-writing is to write down as many important points as you can think of in the story you have been sub-bing, and sooner or later an idea will probably come to you.

3. Some subs are good at hard, up-front headlines; others are better at subtle, punny headlines. Whichever category you fit into – most people are somewhere in the middle – practice certainly makes for punchy headline-writing. On average, a sub on a weekly newspaper should be able to think up a headline in around 5–10 minutes. If in doubt, ask a colleague to help you.

4. Finally, you need to be able to make the headline fit the space that has been allotted for it on the page. You do this by juggling your words around and trying to find shorter (or longer) ones to fit the given space.

Make headlines active

In almost all cases, headlines should have an *active verb*. Occasionally a label headline without a verb is allowed, but this is rare. On some newspapers, label headlines like the following are banned altogether:

CLAMPDOWN ON HIDDEN
COSTS IN MORTGAGES

Labels make headlines dry and inactive. Note also that the second line is too shy. The second line should have been filled out by the sub.

Use a *subject*, *verb* and *object* where you can, so you have a 'Who did What to Whom', such as:

FILM STAR FALLS FOR
MARKET GARDENER

Keep headlines topical
Headlines should be *topical* and up-to-date, as if they have just happened. Always try to put them in the present or future tense.

MAN WINS AWARD FOR
SAVING DROWNING BOY

is better than:

MAN WON AWARD AFTER
SAVING DROWNED BOY

which sounds as if it happened weeks ago.

The only exceptions to this rule are court cases and inquests when deaths and accidents are usually put in the past tense, as they happened months before the hearing.

Keep out those pronouns
Try not to start headings with *it*, *he*, *she* or *they* unless it is an off-beat headline – they are all too impersonal.

Make your heads punchy
Try to keep your headline words short and punchy, unless you are

literally grappling to fill a space and cannot find an alternative. Long words in headlines tend to look clumsy.

Exercise
Put a one-line heading on the following story which appeared in *The Times*.

> Police are investigating the mysterious disappearance of around 4,000 pigeons from London's Trafalgar Square.
>
> A man has been seen trapping up to 50 a day by luring the birds into a box baited with bread-crumbs.
>
> He has told eye-witnesses that the pigeons are for racing, but police believe they are more likely to be found on the tables of London's restaurants.

Straplines and standfirsts

Standfirsts
Important stories and features sometimes need a summary or explanation underneath the headline. This is known as a *standfirst*, the idea being to link the headline to the story. Here is an example of a headline and standfirst.

They've moved the goalposts
UPDATED PLANS FOR HOUSING ESTATE ENRAGE NEIGHBOURS

As you can see, the headline is a bit of a footballing metaphor, while the standfirst neatly links it to the story.

Sometimes the author of the story is included in the standfirst. Here is an example:

Driven to madness

Do not hoot at horses in Romania, or drive your bus anti-clockwise round the Isle of Wight ... **Simon Hacker** tours the globe in search of the more colourful traffic laws

Straplines

The *strapline* is a one-liner that goes above (and occasionally below) a headline and is in smaller type. The strap is used to explain the head in simple English and is commonly used on major news stories.. It is also used to link two stories with simlar themes together, such as:

Banks and building societies face new guidelines to improve consumer protection

Clampdown on hidden costs in mortgages

BY ANDREW VERITY

MORTGAGE LENDERS are poised to announce a clampdown on the controversial practice of offering glittering upfront mortgage deals which gloss over the sting of redemption penalties.

The Council of Mortgage Lenders, which represents all mortgage lenders, including banks, is preparing a big change to the Code of Mortgage Lending in an attempt to tighten rules to prevent customers being hoodwinked.

The clampdown follows an angry debate over the practice of offering very low interest rates in order to tempt customers into buying fixed and discounted mortgages.

Lenders take a loss when they lure borrowers with a very low rate. But there is mounting concern that they fail to explain the sting in the tail: The borrower is bound to a much less beneficial rate a few years later.

The "bargain" rates, especially on some five-year fixed-rate deals, also carry heavy redemption penalties which force the customer to stick with that lender, even when the rate is no longer fixed. The redemption penalties often amount to thousands of pounds.

John Heaps, chief executive of Britannia Building Society, said: "We are looking at rules about how clear lenders make the point that there is a trade-

off. It's not clear that [borrowers] always understand that."

Lenders are required to publish details of redemption penalties in the small print of mortgage contracts, but there is no explicit rule ensuring borrowers understand the link.

Earlier this year, the Building Societies Association began pressing for redemption penalties to be abolished altogether if they extend beyond the period when a mortgage rate is fixed. Lenders backed away after mortgage brokers claimed scrapping the penalties would reduce customer choice.

The code will require lenders to ensure that customers understand the trade-off.

Banks agree code to stop rate 'shrinking'

BY PAUL WALSH
Political Correspondent

BRITAIN'S LEADING banks will today unveil a tough new set of guidelines aimed at ending unfair practices that have left customers thousands of pounds out of pocket.

The new Code of Practice published by the British Bankers' Association (BBA) follows criticism from MPs that some banks had deceived current and savings' account holders by changing interest rates without their knowledge.

The Treasury launched an investigation earlier this year into claims by the Commons Public Accounts Committee that banks had been offering some customers rates as low as 1 per cent on accounts they deemed "obsolete".

The Treasury wanted an end to "shrinking" – the practice where high-interest accounts are launched only to have their rates down-graded or terms changed some months later.

Treasury Minister Helen Liddell ordered an inquiry into the MPs' claims, and threatened that such practices would be made illegal under the forthcoming Financial Services Bill, unless banks sorted out their affairs voluntarily.

Today's BBA Code of Practice promises to offer "fair and reasonable" rates to those whose accounts have been de-

clared obsolete through low use.

It also makes clear that no bank can change the terms and conditions of an account without 30 days written notice and a farther 30-day waiver of any penalty charges incurred when accounts are changed. To ensure that customers can compare rival deals fairly, all interest rates have to be calculated in a standard way.

David Davis, chairman of the Public Accounts Committee, said: "This is a victory for common sense and for customers. If the banks obey not just the letter but the spirit of the code then they will go a long way to winning back the confidence of customers."

Some big news stories or features have a headline, standfirst, by-line and strapline, such as the following example:

The Boat Race: Fun-loving freshman

Light-hearted and light blue

Andrew Longmore
studies the delicate
balancing acts
of Tom Stallard

Captions

Whenever a newspaper or magazine includes a picture, it carries a short description underneath to say what it is about. This is known as a *caption*. Like headline-writing, caption-writing is a creative art. Pictures and illustrations spark the imagination and inspire ideas.

Styles of caption

If you have a scenic or abstract photograph, writing a caption can be an exercise of the imagination. Usually, however, you will be supplied with the basic details, and your job will be to make the words readable and interesting.

Some newspaper features desks (for example, at *The Times* and *Daily Telegraph*) and magazines like their captions to begin with a *bullet*. This is two key words in bold capital letters that set the tone of the piece.

TROUBLED WATERS: Venice's famous Bridge of Sighs was so-called because of
the posses of pining prisoners who travelled across it from a nearby jail.

Another favourite is the *head-and-shoulders* photograph or *pic*,
in which just the person's head and shoulders are shown. These are
usually square, single-column photos with a one- or two-line caption
that includes the subject's name.

Two top tips about captions

Tip one: photographers sometimes jot down a short description on
the back of the photograph (also known as the *pic*) or a piece of
paper. Don't forget they are *snappers* by profession, not *reporters*

(though some photo-journalists are equally adept at writing and photography) – so, as a good sub, always double-check spellings, titles and facts.

Tip two: don't use the same words in the caption bullet and head-line. It looks sloppy.

The by-line and credit

The *by-line* is the name of the journalist who wrote the article. It is usually carried underneath the headline or included in the stand-first. If a story is an exclusive, the by-line may accompany a photograph of the journalist. This is known as a *picture by-line*. Occasionally, for space or design reasons, the journalist's name appears at the foot of the story. In this case it is known as a *sign-off*. Most photographs or illustrations carry the name of the photographer or artist. This is known as the *picture credit* and usually appears in the top right-hand corner of the pic.

Features, sport and business subbing

Subbing is a versatile trade. On larger newspapers, you can work in the news, business, sport, features or arts departments, while on magazines you have even wider scope to deploy your sub-editing skills on subjects from gadgetry to garters. If you are a specialist sub, you need to have an interest in the field you are covering and to know the key technical words and phrases.

Features and arts subbing is more expansive than news, and gives you scope for witty or punny headlines; while, because of its verve and excitement, the average sports desk likes racy, action-packed headlines. The business and City pages tend to mix fact with their fiction and data with their double-entendres!

Designs of the times

Readers of newspapers and magazines tend to be creatures of habit. They know what they want and often buy the same publications on a regular basis. They like to know where to find their favourite columns and articles and to have them presented in a familiar format. It may take months of careful thought before they change their daily or monthly reading diet. This explains why individual circulation figures vary so little from week to week, year on year, and why publications rarely change their design. When the *Guardian* had typographical makeovers in 1988 and 1999, they were heralded as major journalistic events.

Newspapers and magazines strive to make every picture and story distinctive enough to catch the reader's eye. The broadsheets tend to be more discreet, relying on a classical layout. Their news pages are clearly defined in blocks and rectangles, with heavier typefaces giving impact to important news and a more elegant and stylish format for the more eclectic features and entertainment pages. Popular tabloid newspapers print racy headlines and bold pictures to entertain a mass audience, resisting a mordant urge to show galling pictures of torture or death that would simply upset their readers. Magazines are more aesthetic and taste-conscious – the deep, pastoral greens and browns of those such as *Country Life* contrasting vividly with the striking reds, whites and pinks of the younger women's audience.

Layout is a field that needs comprehensive study. Here are a few basic principles to give you a taster.

What layout subs need to know

Some subs have a natural eye for layout. Others gain their skills through practice. It is only by constantly trying out typefaces, space, tinting and colour that you can make the pictures and stories walk proudly off the page.

Here are some useful layout aids:

Minding the drop

The *drop-cap* is the first letter of an article, often blown up to several times its normal size to give impact to bigger news or features stories.

DEJAN Lukic is not good news for the West. Born in the melting pot of Sarajevo, he grew up with Muslim friends, married a Croat, studied oriental languages at university and became a TV newsreader and foreign correspondent. He filed reports from the Middle

There had been so many warnings and so many false alarms that it seemed impossible that anything would actually *happen*. Repeatedly, the West warned Slobodan Milosevic that he must back down if he did not want to face terrible consequences. Repeat-

*L*ate love does not always come singly. In my case I met three eligible men within two years. Curiously all were 10 to 12 years my junior and all lived alone in their own homes within 10 miles of each other on the south coast.

The *drop-quote* (*see* Glossary) is good for breaking up a dense area of grey in longer articles. The text is taken from the story itself.

Between London and Gatwick three privatised operators provide 19 options. The cheapest is £8.30, the most expensive £30.
Before privatisation passengers could choose between first and second class with

'There has to be a better, simpler way'

a cheaper price for off-peak tickets. Now there are 20 options between London and Bristol and a similar number for anyone travelling between the capital and Manchester. The situation is repeated across Britain.

'Cruelty to animals, and wanton indifference to that cruelty, have no place in a civilised society'

"There's actually something exciting about a woman buying you flowers" TOM, 27

Boxing clever

If you look at most broadsheet newspaper pages, you will see that the stories are neatly divided into *boxes* and panels. Some of the tabloids use a more varied format of silhouette, curving copy and *break-outs* (*see* Glossary). A neat way to give stories contrast is to use tints or tones on texts, standfirsts or headlines. These can be in colour or black-and-white. The most popular are referred to as

WOBs (White on Black), *BOTs* (Black on Tint) or *WOTs* (White on Tint).

Capital blitzed by 50 missiles

By ANTONELLA LAZZERI

NATO warplanes pounded the Kosovo capital of Pristina yesterday as the Allies intensified their air campaign.

At least 50 missiles blitzed the area, causing massive damage.

Two main roads were bombed hours after Nato announced the deployment of more aircraft.

The Yugoslav news agency Tanjug said the bombing had caused civilian casualties.

One report claimed a girl of three was killed with her father.

Nato said radar and anti-aircraft missile sites had been targeted along with a special police HQ and fuel dump.

Albania's Foreign Minister Paskal Milo said: "Nato's firm strikes against Milosevic's tyranny are the greatest assistance the Albanians could receive."

Last night the RAF's Harrier heroes teamed up with American A10 "Tankbusters" for twin-pronged strikes.

THE VITAL ADVICE

■ FIT your child's seat carefully following manufacturers' instructions. If you are unsure, phone them for advice.

■ CHECK the seat does not move around when fixed in position. Lean your weight on the seat and tighten the adult seat belt. Ensure it is correctly routed and that the seat belt is not resting against the child seat.

■ ADJUST the harness once your baby is in the seat and allow for the child's clothing. You should be able to slide only two fingers between the harness and your baby's shoulders. Ensure the lower portion of the harness fits across the baby's hips, not across the more vulnerable tummy area.

The finishing touches

Rules and *borders* can give a clean, finished look to page layouts. Borders can be used as picture frames around photographs, illustrations and graphics. They vary from single lines to several overlapping ones. *Rules* are used to divide stories on a page.

Here is an example of a heavy black border on a picture:

It takes all types

There are more than a hundred typefaces used in British newspapers and magazines. These are divided into three distinct styles

- *Roman* for news stories;

- *Bold* for more dramatic stories or presentation;

- *Italic* for a lighter touch (picture captions are often written in italics).

Here are some of the most common typefaces you are likely to come across

New Century Schoolbook:

abcdefghijklmnopqrstuvwxyz
ABCDEFGHIJKLMNOPQRSTUVWXYZ
1234567890

Times Roman:

abcdefghijklmnopqrstuvwxyz
ABCDEFGHIJKLMNOPQRSTUVWXYZ
1234567890

Helvetica:

abcdefghijklmnopqrstuvwxyz
ABCDEFGHIJKLMNOPQRSTUVWXYZ
1234567890

Palatino:

abcdefghijklmnopqrstuvwxyz
ABCDEFGHIJKLMNOPQRSTUVWXYZ
1234567890

Final tip
Try to get as much layout experience as you can when you start your
subbing career. It will certainly pay you dividends in the future.

The story of a 'super sub'

Mike Bradley went into journalism by mistake. After leaving
Downside School, he went to King's College, London, to study for a
German degree. After a year, he realised it was not for him, so he took
a three-year publishing and graphic design diploma course at Oxford
Polytechnic and found it gave him an eye for newspaper design.

However, when Mike left Oxford and moved to London he joined
a bank as a debt collector – 'I was competent enough at the job, but
felt I was wasting the training I had acquired in Oxford,' Mike says
now. Then he saw a job ad in *The Times* for an editor of a small publishing firm. He applied and got the job. With the help of a co-editor,
designer and 40 advertising staff in an open-plan office, Mike produced 23 magazines specialising in such subjects as careers advice,

tourism and London guides. It was a stamina-sapping start to his journalistic career. 'It taught me to be flexible, to be able to do every-thing from simple inputting of text to page layout. I discovered that the ability to be a jack-of-all-trades and muck in with a variety of jobs is a very important priority in sub-editing,' he says.

After two years, he decided to move to a bigger company, joining *Reader's Digest* as a researcher. 'I would sometimes spend two weeks doing background work and fact-checking for one article,' says Mike, who also spent a year in the *Reader's Digest* subs room where he learnt to be meticulous and accurate. He then spotted an advertisement for the chief sub-editor of the *Observer* magazine, spending a year on the Sunday newspaper, before moving to its arch-rival *The Sunday Times* as deputy chief sub of the Arts, Style, Travel and Books sections. 'I enjoyed the creative environment of working on a quality broadsheet and the adrenalin-making ex-perience of working to deadlines. Again, there was an emphasis on accuracy and bringing out a weekly product to a very high standard.'

Mike was a close friend of the journalist Jocelyn Targett, and one day Targett phoned and asked if he would like to help put together a team on a new project, the *Daily Mail*'s Night and Day colour sup-plement, a lively blend of features and interviews. Starting as chief sub, Mike was promoted to commissioning editor, responsible for ideas and liaison with writers. When Targett left, so did Mike, moving back to the *Observer* as TV Editor.

Says Mike: 'If you are good at subbing, you will always be in big demand whether you are a freelance or a full-time employee. You should be adaptable – prepared to work on both magazines and newspapers and learn different computer systems – acquiring a level of competence that will make you more adept at inputting and layout. You may go into a magazine and be asked to design a page on QuarkExpress, for instance. If you can already do this, they are far more likely to ask you to perform other tasks and to work for them again. As with being a reporter, you must be willing to work unsociable hours, and sometimes you will start late mornings or early afternoons, which means you may not get home till midnight. Certainly when deadlines are approaching, you will have to put in extra hours.

'As well as being good at copy-subbing, scrupulous at fact-checking – and, if need be, able to lay out pages, subs need to be adept at re-writing. Some reporters and feature writers are great at discovering the facts and bringing in the details of the story, but not so good at the actual writing. This is where the sub comes in. He or she will have to write or re-write the story to make it readable and in the style of the publication they are working for.'

CHAPTER TEN

The 'Fifth Estate'

A Fleet Street wag recently described the media as the 'Fourth Rate Estate'. He was making a wry comment about a print media that is sometimes dominated by popular tabloid tales of erring ministers, mistresses and misanthropes. Early in the nineteenth century, however, newspapers were referred to by author Thomas Carlyle as the 'Fourth Estate' – the moral guardians of the Government, the Church and the Royal Family.

As it grew bigger, more powerful, and more prone to stray from its Fourth Estate role, the government saw that the media, too, needed a group of moral guardians to keep an eye on its activities. One by one a series of regulators grew up, staffed by members of the media and laymen, to monitor standards of taste and decency. The first was the Press Council in 1953, shortly followed by several television watchdogs, which varied in size and format until the 1990s when five separate bodies were recognised as the guardians of the British media. We shall call them the 'Fifth Estate'.

The Press Complaints Commission
The idea of a Press Complaints Commission sprang from a report by the Calcutt Committee, chaired by Sir David Calcutt, a barrister and Master of Magdalene College, Cambridge. The Committee of 'seven good men and true' was set up in 1990 after a worrying spate of inaccuracies and intrusion by the print media and a general belief by politicians and the establishment that the Fourth Estate really was revealing its Fourth-rate tendencies. In one year alone in the late 1980s, the *Sun* was sued for libel more than fifty times, including a £1 million suit won by the singer Sir Elton John after a series of stories about alleged rent-boy activities. In December 1989, a concerned Andreas Whittam-Smith, founder of the *Independent* newspaper, called a meeting of Fleet Street editors at the World

Trade Centre. During the five-hour session, they devised a Code of Practice for national newspapers and appointed ombudsmen to serve on each paper, ensuring they heeded complaints and inaccuracies and published apologies from dissatisfied customers. The following year, Calcutt reported that newspapers and magazines needed a number of stringent measures to keep them in check. He recommended a new Press Complaints Commission to replace the Press Council that had acted as guardian of the press since 1953. The Commission, headed by Lord McGregor of Durriss, was set up in 1991 with 16 members from journalism, business and public life. Their aim was to uphold press freedom and ethics and to regulate newspapers by rigid use of the editors' Code of Practice. Any individual or organisation that believed their privacy was about to be invaded could phone a Commission hotline and discuss their problems with a member of staff. If the Commission believed the individual's livelihood or reputation were threatened, they could contact the newspaper editor concerned, pointing out the danger and asking them to tread cautiously or drop the story altogether. Whenever there was an error or breach of the Code, the Commission would press the publication's ombudsman to print an apology, issuing an adjudication or ruling over more serious complaints, which it published in the print and broadcasting media.

In 1994, the Commission appointed a Privacy Commissioner, Sir Robert Pinker, a London School of Economics professor. He made his first ruling when Peter Hennessy, a *Mail on Sunday* reporter, managed to get into the home of the Australian author Dr Germaine Greer, after she had placed an advertisement in the *Big Issue* offering to take in anyone who was homeless or incapacitated. Hennessy arrived at her rural house posing as a penniless cripple and stayed for two days before writing about his experiences in the newspaper. Professor Pinker ruled that both journalist and newspaper had breached the Commission's Code of Practice by using 'subterfuge and invasion in pursuit of a story'.

There have been a number of attempts to introduce privacy legislation. Each has failed because politicians are loathe to bring in laws to curb the freedom of the press and its ability to root out corruption among public figures and major criminals. They also fear the media backlash that would follow such a law. Under Lord Wakeham, former chairman of the Tory Party who took the helm in 1994, the PCC has become a more effective watchdog, with at least two revisions of the Code and several warnings to the media over such events as the death of Diana, Princess of Wales, and some intrusive reporting into politicians' private lives.

Among important Code changes have been that newspapers and magazines are not permitted to interview children under the age of 16 without their parents' consent; photographers are not allowed to use long lenses to take pictures of people in private places; and journalists are not permitted to pay the witnesses of current criminal trials for material unless it is in the public interest – neither must they obtain pictures or information by intimidation, harassment or pursuit.

The PCC handles more than 3,000 complaints from individuals and organisations a year, most of which are about inaccuracy caused by careless reporting and poor fact-checking. With intrusion cases, the Commission's main aim is to find whether the story is in the public interest – and therefore *should* be published. A classic example of this argument was the *Sunday Mirror*'s 1997 story about Tory MP Piers Merchant. The MP was caught by a long lens kissing an 18-year-old girl in a park, on a wooden bench and later *de flagrante* in a hotel bedroom. Merchant repeatedly denied the affair, but many believed that if were true, it did not affect his work or responsibilities as an MP and was not therefore in the public interest. Merchant resigned from the Conservative government. There was a surge of similar stories in the 1990s, some of which led to resignations; others, to parliamentary reprimands. It is media pressure, not public interest, that usually forces the issue.

Make your own privacy ruling

Imagine you are a member of the Press Complaints Commission and are asked to adjudicate on the Piers Merchant case. What would your ruling be? Would you decide that the *Sunday Mirror*'s pictures of the MP apparently romping with his mistress on a hotel bed were a case of gross and unnecessary intrusion? Or would you argue that the newspaper was right to print the story and pictures as he was a member of a Government that was advocating family values? Give your ruling and reasons in around 150 words.

A test of your own ethics

While working as a reporter on the *Huddletone Mercury*, you discover your partner's mother, the well-known television actress Carole Court, is having an affair with a junior government minister, while her husband, a senior Bank of England official, is away on European business. Do you:

1. Tell your news editor, so the story can be splashed in all its tabloid glory on the newspaper's front-page?

2. Follow the story up yourself so that, with the aid of a national newspaper contact, you can sell it exclusively to the *News of the World* for £20,000?

3. Ignore the affair altogether?

There is no obvious answer, but you can have great fun comparing notes with your colleagues.

Next, using your sub-editing skills, invent three possible headlines you might put on the story: one local, one tabloid and one broadsheet. Here is an example: 'Carole Court in the Act!'

The Broadcasting Standards Commission

The British dislike censorship. Whenever a new regulator or watchdog is appointed for an industry or profession, there are loud murmurings of discontent and appeals for changes in the law which sometimes border on open revolt. Look at the outcry whenever a British film censor decides to lop a few seconds off a new feature film. 'The Continentals can get away with it, so why can't we?' is the common refrain.

In the 1930s, the idea of censoring the sacred BBC would have been tantamount to a treasonable offence. It was only when commercial television channels and radio stations were introduced in the 1950s and 1960s that the idea of making radio and television accountable to public taste was even considered. Until then, the average broadcaster was able to take a fairly free and unfettered approach to news and programme-making.

Then, suddenly, ITV introduced a violence code. 'Ingenious and unfamiliar methods of inflicting pain and injury – particularly if capable of easy imitation – should not be shown without the most careful consideration,' it said. The first serious signs of broadcasting regulation occurred soon afterwards in 1972, when the BBC set up a three-man commission to hear individual complaints about programmes. The same year, the Independent Broadcasting Authority (IBA) was created to supervise and grant franchises to commercial radio and television networks and monitor 'controversial' issues.

Noting a rise in tasteless programmes, the Labour Government's Annan Committee recommended setting up the Broadcasting Complaints Commission in 1981. Its role was to hear cases of unjust and unfair treatment and invasions of privacy in BBC and commercial programmes and a rising number of complaints about sex, violence, bad language, poor taste and inconvenient scheduling.

Whenever the Commission made a ruling, its findings were published in the *Radio Times* and *TV Times* and on the same channel as the rogue item. Its peak year was 1988 when it received 348 complaints – and made 39 rulings from both individuals and institutions. The same year yet another watchdog, the Broadcasting Standards Council, was set up to monitor programmes and carry out audience research into public attitudes and tastes. With the IBA also watching commercial radio and television, the number of regulators was becoming downright confusing.

To simplify the system, the 1996 Broadcasting Act merged the Broadcasting Complaints Commission and Broadcasting Standards Council into the Broadcasting Standards Commission. The BSC, which is chaired by Lady Elspeth Howe and has 13 members, regulates all radio and television – both BBC and commercial – as well as text, cable, satellite and digital services. Like the Press Complaints Commission, the BSC is not a law court and cannot fine or send broadcasters to prison, but it can call a hearing, at which the complainant, a representative of the broadcaster and other witnesses give their versions of events. It then reaches a verdict. Should the hearing agree with the complaint, it will be upheld, and a copy of the decision sent to the offending broadcaster followed by publication in a monthly bulletin seen by broadcasters, the government and the print media. The BSC can also order the broadcaster to publish its decision on-air at the same time as the original programme went out.

The BSC has two Codes: one on privacy and fairness; the other to monitor taste and decency. One of its main priorities is to ensure that programmes shown before the 9.00 pm watershed are suitable for children. A 1999 survey on sex and families showed 36% of viewers believed there was too much sex on television, with another 56% believing television sex encouraged children to experiment too early in their lives.

The Independent Television Commission

The Independent Television Commission replaced the IBA, after complaints that the latter had become too powerful. An impartial voice with a lighter touch was needed, said the critics. So a new watchdog was born in 1990. Television stations now had to compete for work via public auctions instead of at the IBA's behest. The ITC's role is to license and regulate all commercial television in the UK, including teletext, terrestrial, cable, digital, and satellite services. It also has its own television code and, unlike the PCC and BSC, can fine offending companies.

The ITC's powers are:

- to issue reprimands for minor breaches or genuine mistakes over its Code's terms;

- to give formal warnings, ask for on-screen corrections or apologies, disallow repeats and impose fines over more serious matters;

- to shorten a company's licence or withdraw it altogether in extreme cases of bad taste or unpleasant viewing.

Each year, the ITC reviews television services in an Annual Performance Review. This shows whether programme quality and diversity has or has not been achieved. Its rulings on complaints are published in a monthly report. Recently it received more than 100 complaints from viewers about the Jerry Springer talk-show on the Living and ITV channels. Viewers complained that some programmes began and ended in verbal abuse and violent, on-screen fights between guests. The ITC ruled that due to such violent behaviour the programme was not suitable for showing before the 9.00 pm watershed.

Exercise
What do you think of the Jerry Springer show? Should it be banned or not? Write a 200-word leader in the style of the *Mirror* or a 400-word one in the style of the *Guardian*.

The Radio Authority
The Radio Authority was set up in 1990 to replace the IBA's commercial radio responsibility. It is the watchdog for all national, local, cable, digital, satellite, hospital, community and student radio services. Its main tasks are to organise frequencies so they do not overlap; to regulate programming and advertising; and to appoint licensees that extend the range of local radio services. It has several Codes of Practice and similar powers to the ITC, including sanctions

such as on-air apologies and corrections, fines and the shortening or withdrawal of licences.

The Authority strives to raise radio broadcasting standards. It recently fined one of the new local radio stations, Huddersfield FM, the sum of £5,000 for not maintaining a good enough service for its listeners, including failure to broadcast a topical phone-in, not running education features, inadequate sports coverage and no arts or entertainment features.

The Institute of Public Relations

Britain's first public relations officers were three civil servants who were paid to read the newspapers and pass on what they said to the Treasury in the early nineteenth century. Then, in the 1850s the GPO decided to 'take these black arts of propaganda seriously' and adopted a PR team to give handy postal hints to the general public. The first prime minister to use press officers was Lloyd-George who sent a group of publicity specialists on a nationwide lecture tour to explain the new old-age pension. By the 1930s even King George V saw the value of public relations, recruiting a PRO to write his speeches 'so I don't sound too darned pompous'. In 1948, a group of local government PROs met up and formed a group to 'assist in the establishment of satisfactory status, recruitment and training of future public relations officers.'

It was called the Institute of Public Relations and it first president was Sir Stephen Tallents. A PR pioneer, who had run publicity offices at the GPO, BBC and the Government Overseas Services, Tallents was one of the first PRs to recruit publicists and artists and to bring organisations into the public eye (*see* also Chapter 5, p. 61–62).

Today, the 6,000-strong Institute is the largest body for practising PRs in Europe. Its function is to coordinate, train and regulate its members. It also awards annual Swords of Excellence awards to foster effective PR among members. Like the media watchdogs, the IPR has a Code of Practice to maintain high ethical standards among members, and if an individual or organisation complains about an IPR member, the case goes before a Professional Practices Committee. Should the committee decide there has been a serious breach of the Code, the case will be passed to the Institute's Disciplinary Committee which has the power to reprimand, suspend or dismiss members from the IPR. In 1995, the IPR set up a Register of Members' Interests.

Pressure Groups

There are two main pressure groups who constantly lobby for a responsible and democratic media. They are The PressWise Trust and the Campaign for Freedom of Information.

The PressWise Trust

The PressWise Trust is a small company with a large purpose – to monitor ethics and accuracy in the media. It was founded in 1993 by Clive Soley MP, the present chairman of the Labour Party, after he failed to get his Freedom and Responsiblity of the Press Bill through parliament and thus set up an independent press regulator with statutory powers. The Trust is based largely on the efforts of its full-time executive director Mike Jempson. A former journalist, Jempson is a vocal and compassionate operator, representing victims of media abuse and giving frequent broadcasts and newspaper interviews in his efforts to combat inaccuracy and intrusion. Other campaigners have included Linda Townley, former maid to the Princess Royal who was herself the victim of a media vilification campaign over Royal letters; Pat Healy, the *Independent* and *Times* health writer; and Bill Norris, a former ITN and *Times* correspondent who was also director of the National Union of Journalists.

Funded by the Joesph Rowntree Foundation and the Media Research Trust, PressWise holds seminars on such subjects as race, child exploitation and human rights in the media. It also runs ethical training courses and prints papers on privacy and freedom of expression. It has recently worked on European projects with UNICEF, the International Federation of Journalists and the World Health Organisation.

Campaign for Freedom of Information

Secrets and Lies, the title of British director Mike Leigh's film, neatly sums up the media's often cynical view of British red tape. For some reason, we like to weave a web of intrigue around the activities of our civil service, government institutions and many large companies. Maybe it helps give them an air of mystery and importance. It also creates a dense labyrinth of bureaucracy. A Freedom of Information Act might help to lift this veil.

In 1984, the Campaign for Freedom of Information was created by the Liberal reformer and former Shelter director Des Wilson. Its purpose was to try to give both media and public greater access to government and public institution records and files. The CFI is now supported by 90 like-minded organisations including Friends of the Earth, Greenpeace and a number of trade unions who meet regularly and devise ideas and strategies for the campaign.

A small, non-profit-making group, the CFI successfully drafted and promoted four Private Member's Bills which became law. They were the Access to Personal Files Act (1987), the Access to Medical Reports Act (1988), the Environment and Safety Information Act (1988) – which says all notices served by agencies on public hazards or safety and environmental breaches must be made public – and the 1990 Access to Health Records Act. Then in 1997, the campaign achieved a major breakthrough when 'Your Right To Know', the Government's White Paper on Freedom of Information was published. The following year, a private Freedom of Information Bill was introduced in the House of Lords. Then in 1999, the Freedom of Information Bill was introduced by the Home Office.

Should it become law, the Act will help give media and public alike access to a huge mass of information, ranging from paper and electronic records to unrecorded matter. Facts that are known to officials but not held on file will be also accessible, helping to discourage the deliberate witholding of material. Other currently secret areas that will become public include safety tests on new cars, fire inspections at mainline and underground rail stations and safety reports on projects like the Channel Tunnel.

A perfect example of a project covered by an FOI Act in one country and not in another is the annual inspection of the QE2, which makes regular runs between Southampton and New York. When inspectors went on board to survey the ship, they found dirt-encrusted kitchens and inadequate hygeine throughout, facts they outlined in a special report. When it was published in the USA, which has a Freedom of Information Act, no more was said about it. However when details of the report, which was witheld and deemed secret in the UK, sneaked out of the USA into Britain, it became a big media story.

Glossary

A

ABC Audit Bureau of Circulations, body that authenticates and publishes newspaper and magazine publication figures

Ad Advertisement

Ad dummy Blank set of pages of a newspaper or magazine with the positions of advertisements marked in

Ad rule Rule or border separating editorial matter from advertisements

Add Copy added to a story already written or subbed

Advance Printed handout of a speech or statement issued in advance to the media

Advertising agency Company that prepares and designs advertisements and buys advertising space for clients

Advertorial An article that combines editorial and advertising, usually selling an idea, service or product

Agony aunts *or* **uncles** Journalists who give advice to readers through their columns or readers' correspondences

Alts Alterations made to a story

Apology When a newspaper or magazine admits an error and prints an apology

Angle A particular approach to a story

AP Associated Press, American news agency that sends foreign copy to newspapers

Artwork Design and layout of pages (mostly done on computer)

Ascender That part of a letter above its x-height, i.e. ie. h k l and f (*see* also Descender)

Assignment Story a journalist or correspondent has been asked to cover

Attribution Linking information or quotations in an article to their original source

Author's marks Corrections or changes made by a writer on a story or article

B

Backbench Executive journalists on a newspaper who decide the day's or week's format

Background piece Article exploring the background features of a news story

Back numbers Previous issues of a newspaper or magazine

Back-up Fall-back system of news copy on a computer

Banner Front-page headline that runs across the page. Also known as a *streamer*

Bastard setting Typesetting of non-standard width

Big quotes Quotation marks larger than the type they enclose, used for emphasis in an article

Bill Newsstand poster bearing the day's main headlines

Black Electronic duplicate of a story

Blob Solid black orb used for emphasis

Blow-up Enlargement of a picture or type

Blurb Copy about a new product or the content of an article or page written to attract readers

Body Copy in a story that follows the intro

Bold Thick or heavy typeface used for emphasis or contrast

Border Rule or line used to separate or make panels for stories

BOT Layout expert's term meaning black print on a toned background (*see* also WOB and WOT)

Box Story with rules on all four sides

Break Convenient place to insert a quote or cross-head in a story's text

Breaker Any device such as a panel, quote or cross-head which breaks up the text in a page

Breaking story Story that is happening now

Break-out Secondary story to the main one on a page

Brief News editor's instructions for going on a story, sometimes known as a *briefing*; short, one- or two-paragraph story

Broadsheet Large-size newspaper such as *The Times*, the *Guardian*, the *Independent*, the *Daily Telegraph* and *The Financial Times*

Bucket Print rules that tie a caption to a picture

Columns   Vertical divisions of a newspaper or magazine

Column rule   Line between columns of type

Command   Keyboard instruction

Contacts book   The good journalist's bible. Address book containing names and numbers of useful contacts

Content   Editorial in a newspaper or magazine

Contents bill   Bill or poster advertising a newspaper's top stories

Copy   Material submitted to a newspaper or magazine (*see* Hard copy)

Copy and paste   When a sub-editor moves type from one file to another

Copyright   Ownership of printed or written material

Copytaker   Person who takes down incoming stories from reporters

Copy-taster   Senior sub-editor who checks, selects or discards copy

Correction   Item putting right a mistake that appeared in a newspaper or magazine

Correspondent   Specialist (for example, defence, environment, rugby correspondent) or foreign reporter on a newspaper, magazine or broadcast network

Coverage   Attendance at news events

Credit   Photographer's or illustrator's name, usually printed in the top right-hand corner of a picture

Crop   Cut a picture to size

Crosshead   Line of type (usually one or two words) to break the text in a story

Cross-ref   Cross-reference, sentence at the bottom of a story that refers to another item in a newspaper or magazine

Cub   Trainee reporter

Cursor   Small square or arrow used to pinpoint text on a computer screen

Cut   Reduce a story by deleting text

Cut-off   Story separated from the text by rules

Cut-out   Removing a photograph's background to form a silhouette

Cuttings   Newspaper or magazine stories filed in a library or kept in a personal cuttings book

Bullet   Two-word start of a picture caption, for emphasis

Bureau   Office of a news agency; overseas office of a newspaper

Bury   When important information is hidden in the text of a story

Bust   When a headline has too many characters for the space allotted to it

By-line   Name of the journalist at the top of a story (referred to as a *sign-off* when it appears at the bottom of a story)

C

Calls   Routine calls made by reporters to police, fire, ambulance and coastguards to see if there is any recent news

Caps   Capital letters of type

Caption   Words used underneath a photograph or illustration

Cast off   Edit a story to a fixed length

Casual   Journalist who works for a newspaper, magazine or network on a temporary basis

Catchline   Word summing up a story that is used for identification

CD-Rom   Compact disc holding useful data

Centre spread   Copy and pictures covering the two middle pages of a newspaper or magazine

Centred   Type equidistant from each side of a column or columns

Chapel   In-house branch of a union

Character   Word or figure of type

Chequebook journalism   Stories a newspaper pays for – usually scandals about celebrities, politicians or mistresses. When several newspapers compete for the same story, an *auction* is held

Chief sub-editor   Usually referred to as the Chief Sub who supervises the sub-editors' desk

Circulation figures   Number of copies of a newspaper or magazine sold. Usually verified by the ABC (*see* above)

City desk   Section of a newspaper that handles city and business news

Classified ads   Small advertisements listed in columns and sections, but not displayed (*see* Display advertisements)

Clip   Short extract from an interview

Colour piece   Story written as a descriptive or background piece after a news event

D

Database   Store of electronic data

Dateline   Date and place of a story

Deadline   Latest time a story can be accepted for an edition

Deck   One line of a headline

Delete   Cut or remove copy

Demo-tape   Collection of taped reports for job applications

Descender   The part of a letter that falls below the x-line, such as g, j, p, q and y (*see* also Ascender)

Diary   Book containing the day's or week's jobs

Diary piece   Item of light-hearted or celebrity news that goes in a diary column

Directory   List of stories held in a computer

Disclaimer   Apology pointing out that the names or organisations mentioned in a story are incorrect

Display ads   Large, eye-catching advertisements (*see* Classified Ads)

Doorstepping   Reporters or photographers pursuing sources by waiting outside their homes or institutions (sometimes literally on the doorstep, hence the phrase)

Downtable subs   Team of sub-editors below chief and deputy chief sub-editor level

Drop-cap   Big capital letter at the start of a story

Drop-quotes   Big quotes used to emphasise important features in a story

Dubbing   Mixing of various film sound tracks

Dummy   Mock-up of a newspaper or magazine

E

Edit   Cut, re-write and prepare copy/tapes/film/videos for publication or air-time

Edition   Issue of a newspaper or magazine brought out at a specific time or for a given area

Editor   Person in overall charge of a newspaper or magazine; person responsible for organising and editing news in radio or television

Editor's conference   Meeting of news executives who plan the day's or week's news

Editorial   All non-advertising copy in a newspaper or magazine; leading article or opinion piece giving a newspaper's views (*see* Leader)

E-mail   Electronic mail sent via computer

Embargo   Request not to publish or put on air an article or press release before a specific time

Exclusive   Scoop or big-impact story obtained by a newspaper reporter (*see* Scoop)

F

Feature   Descriptive article based on a topic of interest or background to the news

File   Send story from a foreign country

Files   Back issues of a newspaper or magazine

Filler   Short news item, one or two paragraphs long

Fleet Street   Traditional term for Britain's national newspaper industry, so named as nearly all of them were based in or around Fleet Street, near Blackfriars Bridge and on the fringes of the City of London

Flush   Set type to one side (i.e., flush left or right)

Follow-up   News story that follows up another one

Fount   Typeface of a given size and style

Fourth Estate   Nineteenth century name given to the press when it was seen as the moral guardian of the monarchy, government and church. The phrase is attributed to the historian Thomas Carlyle in 1837

Freebie   Free meal, visit or gift given to a journalist by a company as a goodwill gesture

Freelance   Self-employed journalist who works for several companies

Free newspaper   Newspaper that relies on advertising for its income, has no cover price and is usually delivered to households

Full out   When a line of print covers a whole column without indentation

G

Ghost writer   Journalist who writes a book for someone else, usually a celebrity, and under their name

Graphics Drawings or illustrations used in page design

Gutter Margin between two printed pages

H

Hack Slang term for a journalist

Handout Copy of a speech or announcement for use by a journalist

Hanging indent When the first line of a story is set full out and the remaining lines indented on the left

Hard copy Printed or handwritten material, used to as a back-up to inputted copy

Hard news Straight, factual reports

Head and shoulders Small photograph showing subject's head (*see* Mug Shot)

Headline Title of a news or features story, sometimes known as *head* or *heading*

House style Phrases and spelling adopted as standard practice on a newspaper or magazine

Human interest Story with a human angle

I

In camera Court cases and inquests may be held behind closed doors when highly sensitive or confidentiual matter is being discussed

Imprint Name and address of the printer and publisher, usually printed at the foot of a newspaper's back page or inside the cover of a magazine

Indent A line of print inset at the beginning or end

Index Front-page list of main stories in a newspaper

Input Type copy into a computer

Insert Copy put into an article after it is written

Internet International computer network based on websites

Intro First paragraph of a story or article

Investigative journalism In-depth reporting used to expose corrupt or suspicious practices

Issue Edition of a newspaper or magazine

J

Journalese   Newspaper or magazine slang

K

Kill   Erase or spike a story

L

Label   Headline with no verb that appears like a title ie. Vicar in accident (instead of Vicar hurt in accident)
Lawyer   In-house expert who checks legal problems in stories
Layout   Page design
Lead   Reporters follow up a lead, or angle, in a story; main story on a page, sometimes referred to as the *page lead*
Leader   Main editorial giving a newspaper's views on a current topic (*see* Editorial)
Leg   Portion of text arranged in several columns
Legal   Check a story for legal problems such as libel or contempt of court
Lift   Use a story from another publication or previous edition
Lineage   Payment to freelances for stories, based on the number of lines used
Literals   Inputting errors
Lobby   Specialist group of correspondents covering parliament
Long lens   Photographer's telescopic lens (*see* Telephoto lens)
Lower case   Small, as opposed to capital, letters (*see* Upper case)

M

Make-up   Page planning
Masthead   Newsaper's title at the top of page one
Measure   Width of any setting
MF   initials at the foot of a page to show that more follows
Middle-market   Middle-of-the-range tabloids such as the *Daily Mail* and *Express* that appeal to the middle-classes

Modem   Telephone link that joins computers to e-mail and Internet

Mug shot   Photograph showing subject's head (*see* Head and Shoulders)

N

Nationals   Britain's national daily and Sunday newspapers

NCTJ   National Council for the Training of Journalists, the journalists' training body

News agency   Organisation that reports and sells news to newspapers, radio and television

News desk   Nerve centre where news is organised and collected

NIB   News in brief, a one-paragraph story (*see* Shorts)

Night editor   Newspaper's senior production editor

Nose   Intro or first paragraph of a story

Nugget   Small item of news

NUJ   National Union of Journalists, the main journalists' union

O

Obit   Short for obituary

Off-beat story   One that gives a wry or humorous view of an event

Off-the-record   Comments or statements that are not for publication

On spec   Story or article sent in by a freelance that has not been commissioned

Op-ed   Any story that appears on the page opposite the editorial

Opinion piece   Article that contains a journalist's views

Orphan   Short, clumsy-looking line at the foot of a column that sub-editors are told to avoid (*see* Widow)

P

PA   Press Association, Britain's main home news, sport, finance and features agency

Package   Number of radio wraps joined together

Pagination   Numbering of pages
Panel   Story enclosed in rules or borders
Paparazzi   Pack of photographers
Par   Abbreviation for paragraph
Pay-off   End of a news bulletin
Pic   Abbreviation for photograph
Picture desk   Section of a publication that produces and organises photographs
Pool   Select group of journalists with special access to an event
Populars   Mass circulation tabloid newspapers
PR   Public relations
Press release   Printed handout about an event for publication in the media
Print-out   Copy of printed material used for reference
Print-run   Total number of newspapers or magazines printed at one time
PRO   Public relations officer, a person who practises public relations
Production editor   Newspaper or magazine executive in charge of production
Proof   Early copy of an edition, page or story
Puff   Item publicising an event
Promotion   Planned publicity with a specific aim
Publics   PR term for audiences that are important to an organisation
Pull-out   Separate section of a publication held inside the main one
Pundit   Popular commentator
Punchline   Main point or angle of a story

Q

Qualities   Serious broadsheet newspapers
Quotes   Abbreviation for quotations
Qwerty   Standard keyboard layout, based on the first five letters of the keyboard

R

Ragged   Copy that is uneven on one side, hence ragged left or ragged right

Red-top   Mass-circulation tabloid newspapers
Re-jib   Revise story after new material has been added
Re-nose   Use a new intro with a different angle
Revise   To check edited material
Re-write   When a sub-editor rewrites a journalist's story
Roman   A standard typeface
Rule   Print border of varying width
Runner   Person who runs errands on a film- or programme-set
Running story   Live story that keeps having fresh developments
Rushes   Raw video footage ready to be cut into a finished report or documentary; urgent news agency copy

S

Scoop   Exclusive story obtained by a reporter
Short   One- or two-paragraph news item
Showreel   Video of your own work for job applications
Sidebar   Story next to and linked to a bigger one
Sign-off   Journalist's name at foot of story (*see* Byline)
Silly season   Period in August when there is little news due to holidays; school and university vacations; and the parliamentary recess
Snapper   Newspaper slang for photographer
Spike   Erase copy or other information
Splash   Main front-page news story
Spread   Main story covering two pages (*see* Centre spread)
Standfirst   Text linking a headline to a story
Stet   Dotted lines under deleted text meaning 'please restore'
Strapline   Explanatory line above or below a headline
Stringer   Freelance journalist in an area or country who supplies copy to the media
Sub-editor   Person who checks and edits journalists' copy
Sub-head   Small heading in the middle of a story
Sub judice   Details of an item that cannot be revealed as they are about to be heard in court (Latin for 'before the law')
Syndication   Material offered for use in a number of publications

T

Tabloid   Compact newspaper that is half the size of a broadsheet

Take   Part of a sequence of up-dated information in a story
Taste   Check, select or discard copy (*see* Copy-taster)
Telephoto lens   Photographer's telescopic lens (*see* Long lens)
Think piece   Thought-provoking article
Tie-in   Story connected to one beside it
Tip-off   Information given to a journalist by an inside source
Top   Story at the top of a page
Trim   Cut a story

U

Underscore   Line or rule under type
Update   Include later information
Upper case   Capital letters as opposed to smaller letters (*see* Lower Case)

V

VDU   Visual Display Unit
Verbatim   Quoting somebody word-for-word
Voicer   Introduction to a radio reporter's story
Vox pop   Short for *vox populi*, street survey of a topical news item

W

Whistleblower   Person who reveals secret information to the media
Widow   Short line left hanging at the top of a column that subs are asked to avoid (*see* Orphan)
Wild track   Raw sound such as diggers on a building site or police sirens used to add colour to a radio, TV or video report
Wire   Transmitting copy by electric signal
WOB   Layout expert's term meaning white print on a black background
WOT   Layout expert's term meaning white print on a tone background (*see* BOT)
Wrap   Radio report introduced by a newsreader

Useful Contacts

THE PRINT MEDIA

National Newspapers

Daily Mail, Northcliffe House, 2 Derry Street, Kensington, London W8 5TT (*tel* 020 7938 6000)

Daily Star, Ludgate House, 245 Blackfriars Road, London SE1 9UX (*tel* 020 7928 8000)

The Daily Telegraph, 1 Canada Square, Canary Wharf, London E14 5DT (*tel* 020 7538 5000)

The Express, Ludgate House, 245 Blackfriars Road, London SE1 9UX (*tel* 020 7928 8000)

Financial Times, 1 Southwark Bridge, London SE1 9HL (*tel* 020 7873 3000)

The Guardian, 119 Farringdon Road, London EC1R 3ER (*tel* 020 7278 2332)

The Independent, 1 Canada Square, Canary Wharf, London E14 5DL (*tel* 020 7293 2000)

Independent on Sunday, 1 Canada Square, Canary Wharf, London E14 5DL (*tel* 020 7293 2000)

The Mail on Sunday, Northcliffe House, 2 Derry Street, Kensington, London W8 5TS (*tel* 020 7938 6000)

The Mirror, 1 Canada Square, Canary Wharf, London E14 5AP (*tel* 020 7293 3000)

Morning Star, 1–3 Ardleigh Road, London N1 4HS (*tel* 020 7254 0033)

News of the World, 1 Virginia Street, London E1 9XR (*tel* 020 7782 4000)

The Observer, 119 Farringdon Road, London EC1R 3ER (*tel* 020 7278 2332)

The Sun, 1 Virginia Street, London E1 9BD (*tel* 020 7782 4000)

The Sunday Express, Ludgate House, 245 Blackfriars Road, London SE1 9UX (*tel* 020 7928 8000)

Sunday Mirror, 1 Canada Square, Canary Wharf, London E14 5AP (*tel* 020 7293 3000)
Sunday People, 1 Canada Square, Canary Wharf, London E14 5AP (*tel* 020 7293 3201)
Sunday Telegraph, 1 Canada Square, Canary Wharf, London E14 5DT (*tel* 020 7538 5000)
The Sunday Times, 1 Pennington Street, London E1 9XW (*tel* 020 7782 5000)
The Times, 1 Pennington Street, London E1 9XN (*tel* 020 7782 5000)

National News Agencies

Press Association, PA Newscentre, 292 Vauxhall Bridge Road, London SW1V 1AA (*tel* 020 7963 7000)
National news, sport, features and business agency supplying newspapers, news organisations, broadcasters and internet users.
Reuters, 85 Fleet Street, London EC4P 4AJ (*tel* 020 7250 1122)
International news agency for newspapers, broadcasters and internet users.

Unions

British Association of Journalists, 88 Fleet Street, London EC4Y 1PJ (*tel* 020 7353 3003)
Chartered Institute of Journalists, 2 Dock Offices, Surey Quays Road, London SE16 2XU (*tel* 020 7252 1187 *or* www.cioj.dircon.co.uk\)
National Union of Journalists, 314–320 Grays Inn Road, London WC1X 8DP (*tel* 020 7278 7916 *or* www.n.apc.org/media/nuj.html)
Publishes an excellent 18-page brochure on jobs and journalism.

Support Organisations

British Society of Magazine Editors, c/o Gill Branston & Associates, 137 Hale Lane, Edgware, Middlesex HA8 9QP (*tel* 020 7906 4664) Professional association for magazine editors and senior editorial staff.
Campaign for Freedom of Information, 88 Old Street, London EC1V 9AX (*tel* 020 7831 7477 *or* www.cfoi.org.uk)
Guild of Editors, University Centre, Granta Place, Mill Lane, Cambridge CB2 1RU (*tel* 01223 304080). Professional association for newspaper editors, editorial directors and training editors.

London Press Club, European Centre, Stanhope House, Stanhope Place, London W2 2HH (*tel* 020 7402 2566 *or* see pressclub@aol.com).

National Readership Surveys, 42 Drury Lane, London WC2B 5RT (*tel* 020 7632 2915) The NRS measures newspaper and magazine readerships.

Newspaper Library, Colindale Avenue, London NW9 5HE (*tel* 020 7412 7353) Cuttings of national, regional and local newspapers, with photocopying, photography and microfilm services.

Newspaper Publishers Association, 34 Southwark Bridge Road, London SE1 9EU (*tel* 020 7928 6928) Trade association for publishers of national newspapers.

Newspaper Society, 74 Great Russell Street, London WC1B 3DA (*tel* 020 7636 7014) Trade association for publishers of local newspapers.

Periodical Publishers Association, 28 Kingsway, London WC2B 6JR (*tel* 020 7404 4166 *or* www.ppa.co.uk) Trade association for magazine publishers.

Press Complaints Commission, 1 Salisbury Square, London EC4 8AE (*tel* 020 7353 1248 *or* www.pcc.org.uk) Regulatory body for the print media. Receives complaints about the content and conduct of newspapers and magazines.

The PressWise Trust, 25 Easton Business Centre, Felix Road, Bristol BS5 OHE (*tel* 0117 941 5889, *fax* 0117 941 5848 *or* pw@presswise.org.uk) Charitable trust that helps victims of unfair, irresponsible or inaccurate media reporting.

Celebrity Contacts

ICM Ltd (International Creative Management), Oxford House, 76 Oxford Street, London W1N 0AX (*tel* 020 7636 6565)

The Stage Newspaper, 47 Bermondsey Street, London SE1 3XT (*tel* 020 7403 1818 *or* info@thestage.co.uk)

Training Bodies

National Council for the Training of Journalists, Latton Bush Centre, Southern Way, Harlow, Essex CM18 7BL (*tel* 01279 430009 *or* www.itecharlow.co.uk.nctj/) The main training body for newspapers. Accredits NCE (National Certificate Examination) and NVQ courses and short courses for journalists. First point of contact for those who want to know about newspaper journalism courses. It publishes a useful careers leaflet and a list of approved pre-entry courses.

Periodicals Training Council, Queen's House, 28 Kingsway, London WC2B 6JR (*tel* 020 7404 4168 *or* www.ppa.co.uk) The main contact for those wishing to train for magazine journalism, it publishes an annual *Directory of Magazine Training* and an invaluable booklet, *A Career in Magazines*, which has a list of approved courses, advice and phone numbers.

UCAS, Rose Hill, New Barn Lane, Cheltenham GL52 3LZ (*tel* 01242 222444 *or* www.ucas.co.uk) Publishes *A Students' Guide to Entry to Media Studies* (£10) which covers postgraduate training courses.

BROADCASTING

Job seeking

BBC Recruitment Services, PO Box 7000 London W12 8GJ (*tel* 020 8740 0005) For information about BBC jobs contact : www.bbc.co.uk/jobs.

BSkyB, Grant Way, Isleworth, Middlesex. TW7 5QD (*tel* 020 7705 3000 *or* www.sjy.co.uk)

Channel 4 Television, 124 Horseferry Road, London SW1P 2TX (*tel* 020 7396 4444 *or* www.channel4.com)

Channel 5 Broadcasting, 22 Long Acre, London WC2E 9LY (*tel* 0345 050505)

Community Media Association, The Media Centre, 15 Paternoster Row, Sheffield S1 2BX (*tel* 0114 279 5219) A non-profit-making organisation that provides training, support, advice and consultancy for community radio and television projects.

Hospital Broadcasting Association, Staithe House, Russel Street, Falkirk FK2 7HP (*tel* 01283 561111) Voluntary organisation that can supply details and advice about almost 300 hospital radio stations in the UK.

ITV Network Centre, 200 Gray's Inn Road, London WC1X 8HF (*tel* 020 7843 8000 *or* www.itv.co.uk) for information about jobs in ITV or ITN.

Radio Authority, 14 Great Queen Street, London WC2B 5DG (*tel* 020 7430 2724 *or* www.radio-authority.org.uk) Publishes *Careers in Broadcasting*, an information and advice fact-sheet, and a Pocket

Book with addresses and phone numbers of all commercial non-BBC radio stations and news services (see regulators).

The Research Register, 47 Anson Road, London N7 0AR (*tel* 020 7700 7573, *fax* 020 7760 2627 *or* www.itv.co.uk).
Agents for television jobs ranging from researchers to directors.

Student Radio Association, 5 Market Place, London W1N 7AH (*tel* 020 7255 2010 and www.radacad.demon.co.uk) Promotes and supports student radio stations and runs conferences, training weekends and student radio awards. Its annual conference is attended by many radio industry executives seeking fresh talent.

Training bodies

BBC Centre for Broadcast Skills Training, Wood Norton, Evesham, Worcestershire WR11 4TB (*tel* 01386 420216 *or* www.bbc.co.uk/training)

British Film Institute, 21 Stephen Street, London W1P 2LN (*tel* 020 7255 1444 *or* www.bfi.org.uk) Publishes a list of broadcasting courses called *Media Course UK* at £10.99. Also carries copies of *The Knowledge*. *PACT* (Producers' Alliance for Cinema and Television) *Directory*, which lists names of all television production companies can be obtained from its library and also public libraries. Houses the National Film and Television Archive – a large collection of TV documentary and feature films.

Broadcast Journalism Training Council, 39 Westbourne Gardens, London W2 5NR (*tel* 020 7727 9522) A list of 16 approved radio journalism courses is on www.bjtc.org.uk

National Film and Television School, Beaconsfield Studios, Station Road, Beaconsfield, Bucks HP9 1LG (tel 01494 671234 *or* www.nftsfilm–tv.ac.uk) Supplies information and booklets and runs a one-year postgraduate course for television.

Skillset, 91–101 Oxford Street, London W1R 1RA (*tel* 020 7534 5300) Training body and pioneer for broadcasters, managed and funded by the BBC, Channel 4 and the ITVA trading associations. Publishes *A Career in Broadcast, Film and Video* on www.skillset.org

UCAS, Rose Hill, New Barn Lane, Cheltenham, GL52 3LZ (*tel* 01242 222444 *or* www.ucas.co.uk). Publishes *A Student's Guide to Entry to Media Studies* (£10) which covers postgraduate training courses.

Agencies

Associated Press Television News, Interchange, 32 Oval Road, Camden Lock, London NW1 7EP (*tel* 020 7410 5200) International news agency for broadcasters which also has one of the most comprehensive film and video archives.

Reuters Television, 200 Grays Inn Road, London WC1X 8XZ (*tel* 020 7250 1122) News agency that supplies broadcasters.

Support groups

British Library National Sound Archive, 29 Exhibition Road, London SW7 2AS (*tel* 020 7412 7440) National collection of sound recording, includes library, information, listening and transcription services.

Royal Television Society, Holborn Hall, 100 Gray's Inn Road, London WC1X 8AL (*tel* 020 7430 1000) Find out about workshops and master-classes for newcomers and experienced alike on info@rts.org.uk. Special membership rates for students.

Regulators

Broadcasting Standards Commission, 7 The Sanctuary, London SW1P 3JS (*tel* 020 7233 0544 *or* www.bsc.org.uk) Statutory body that monitors and considers complaints about inaccurate, unpleasant or offensive television and radio programmes.

Independent Television Commission, 33 Foley Street, London W1P 7LB (*tel* 020 7255 3000 *or* www.itc.org.uk) Public body responsible for licensing and regulating commercial television, cable, satellite and digital services.

Radio Authority, 14 Great Queen Street, London WC2B 5DG (*tel* 020 7430 2724 *or* ww.radioauthority.org.uk) Statutory body that licenses and regulates all non-BBC radio services (*see* also Job Seeking, p. 162).

PUBLIC RELATIONS

Training and support bodies

Communications Advertising Marketing Foundation (CAM), Abford House, 15 Walton Road, London SW1V 1NJ (*tel* 020 7828 7506 *or* www.cam.uk.com) Has a Certificate and Diploma in PR and

Advertising that are taught part-time in adult and FE colleges or by distance learning.

Institute of Public Relations, The Old Trading House, 15 Northburgh Street, London EC1V OPR (*tel* 020 7253 5151 *or* info@ipr1.demon.co.uk and http://www.ipr.press.net) Main support body for the industry. The IPR publishes careers advice and recommended courses. Also has its own Diploma in Public Relations. It publishes a *Getting into Public Relations* pack and organises career days.

The Public Relations Consultants Association, Willow House, Willow Place, London SW1P 1JH (*tel* 020 7523 6026 *or* www.prca.org.uk) Publishes information on job opportunities in PR consultancies. It runs a service for PR jobhunters called Jobseek.

Selective Bibliography

The BBC: 70 Years of Broadcasting (John Cain) BBC
The British Press and Broadcasting since 1945 (Colin Seymour-Ure) Blackwell
Careers in Journalism (Peter Medina and Allan Shepherd) Kogan Page
Cassandra at his Finest and Funniest (Sir William Connor) Hamlyn
How to Get Into Films and TV (Robert Angell) How To Books
Magazine Journalism (John Wharton) Periodicals Training Council
Modern Newspaper Practice (F W Hodgson) Focal Press
The Newspapers Handbook (Richard Keeble) Routledge
Power Without Responsiblity (James Curran and Jean Seaton) Routledge
The Prying Game (Christopher Browne) Robson Books
Teach Yourself Public Relations (J Harvey Smith) Hodder and Stoughton
Understanding Radio (Andrew Crisell) Routledge
The Way to Write Magazine Articles (John Hines) Elm Tree Books
Writing Feature Articles (Brendan Hennessy) Focal Press

Appendix 1

Page No. 103

Suggested questions
How old are you?
Where did you go to school?
Where do you live?
How long have you been acting?
Why do you like acting?
How did you get the West End part?
Are you excited?
Do you have a boyfriend?
What does he think about your new role?
What have your mates said at work?
Do you want to be a full-time actor?

Other good people to interview:
Boyfriend
Parents/brothers/sisters
A factory colleague/s
The factory manager
The talent scout who discovered her
Josie's ex-school head
Play's director
Amateur acting colleagues

Suggested photographs:
*Josie at work in the factory next to a picture of her acting
*Picture of her rehearsing with a cast member (preferably well-known) for the West End musical

These are just suggestions – you may well be able to do better!

Appendix 2

Page No. 122

The list of errors:
MAZE not maize (line one)
ATTRACTION not atraction (line three)
RECESSES not receses (line four)
RIVERSCAPE'. Inside not outside quotes (line five)
PALACE not palice (line six)
MAZE not maize (line six)
LANDMARK not lanmark (line seven)
MAZE not maize (line eight)
WILLIAM not Wiliam (line eight)
CHAINSAW not Chainsore (line nine)
RECOMMENDING not recomending (line ten)
SHALE not shail (line ten)
YEW TREES not you trees (line eleven)
EYESORE not eyesaw (line twelve)
EYESORE'. Inside not outside quotes (line twelve)

Index